Year-Round Education

Change and Choice for Schools and Teachers

Shelly Gismondi Haser
Ilham Nasser

SCARECROWEDUCATION
Lanham, Maryland • Toronto • Oxford
2005

KH

Published in the United States of America
by ScarecrowEducation
An imprint of The Rowman & Littlefield Publishing Group, Inc.
4501 Forbes Boulevard, Suite 200, Lanham, Maryland 20706
www.scarecroweducation.com

PO Box 317
Oxford
OX2 9RU, UK

British Library Cataloguing in Publication Information Available

Library of Congress Cataloging-in-Publication Data

Haser, Shelly Gismondi, 1965–
    Year-round education : change and choice for schools and teachers /
Shelly Gismondi Haser, Ilham Nasser.
        p.   cm.
    Includes bibliographical references and index.
    ISBN 1-57886-235-3 (pbk. : alk. paper)
    1. School year—Virginia—Fairfax County—Case studies.   2. Public
schools—Virginia—Fairfax County—Case studies.   I. Nasser, Ilham,
1963–   II. Title.
LB3034.H37 2005
371.2'36'0973—dc22   2004026683

∞ ™ The paper used in this publication meets the minimum requirements of
American National Standard for Information Sciences—Permanence of Paper
for Printed Library Materials, ANSI/NISO Z39.48-1992. Manufactured in the
United States of America.

12/13/05

Vision is not enough.
It must be combined with venture.
It is not enough to stare up the steps;
we must step up the stairs.

Vaclav Havel

Contents

Foreword

Dan Domenech

When I arrived in Fairfax in December of 1997, the seeds for year-round schools had already been planted in the school system. For my part, prior to my arrival as Fairfax's superintendent of schools, I had visited year-round schools in Hawaii and was intrigued by the notion. I was already convinced that the traditional school calendar had long ago outlived its original purpose, if that purpose was indeed to allow the children in agrarian times to work the fields during the summer months. I also bought into the notion that a two-month absence from school was not beneficial to the learning process and that it had its most adverse effect on children of poverty.

The schools I visited in Hawaii and most of the year-round schools I had read about, however, were devised as solutions to facilities issues rather than as educational solutions. In those cases, the school buildings were overcrowded and a year-round schedule allowed for as much as a 25 percent increase in enrollment. Generally, the children did not spend any more time in school. It just allowed for more children to be in the school. It was also clear that, in most cases where year-round schools were being implemented, the schedule was not popular with any of the members of the school community. It was simply an expedient solution to a space issue.

So, when I was first approached by the principal of one of our elementary schools in Fairfax with the idea of implementing a "modified calendar" school, my first question was, why? I was pleasantly surprised to learn that the idea was being advocated as an educational solution rather than a facilities answer. The intent was not to accommodate more children, but rather to better serve the children that were already in the school. The proposed calendar would begin the school year in late July and proceed through four nine-week semesters with a three-week intersession between semesters. However, two weeks out of the three-week intersession period would be filled with school programs ranging from remediation to enrichment classes for the students. Attendance at these sessions would be voluntary. Given the demographics of the student population at the school, a high percentage of children on free and reduced lunch, it was a good bet that the working parents would want their children attending these two-week sessions, thus assuring those students of as much as thirty more days of school.

One of my priorities upon arriving as Fairfax's new superintendent was to tackle the growing achievement gap between our majority and minority students. One of my strategies was to increase contact time for our underachieving students. Clearly, if students were to catch up to their high-achieving peers, they would have to spend more time in school. After-school programs, Saturday programs, and summer school were traditional approaches. The modified calendar approach seemed like another opportunity. I immediately liked the idea.

Experienced superintendents have learned, usually the hard way, that a good idea is not necessarily an implementable idea. I was already aware of the many challenges faced by year-round schools. The modified calendar presented some additional challenges. First of all, it would cost more money. Year-round schools were generally implemented to save money. Rather than building an annex or a new school, you adopted a year-round schedule and saved a bundle on facilities costs. The modified calendar was not designed to enroll more students and the intersession sessions would be costly, not to mention additional costs for transportation, custodial, secretarial, and many other charges. Second, getting parents, students, and staff to buy into this new schedule would be a significant adaptive challenge. All the other schools would be on the traditional schedule. Siblings would be in and out of school at different times. Staff would be out of sync with the schedules of their own children and of family members who might work in traditional-schedule schools.

Fortunately, the principal was aware of all of these challenges and was willing to take them on. I was impressed by her enthusiasm and her confidence in her ability to sell the idea to her staff and parents. For my part, I was willing to support her and to do my part with the school board. It was an uphill battle, but the concept was sold on its merits as an idea that would significantly improve the achievement levels of the children attending the school. It was another weapon in the fight to close the achievement gap.

The initial evaluation of the modified calendar school in Fairfax showed that student achievement did improve. Over 70 percent of the students attended the intersession sessions. Parents, students, and staff were pleased with the schedule. Consequently, the model was expanded to additional elementary schools in the county as well as to one middle school and one high school. This book is the product of two years of research by Dr. Shelly Gismondi Haser and Dr. Ilham Nasser in three of our modified-calendar elementary schools. They focused on the benefits of the modified-calendar schools for teachers. It was clear to the designers of the modified calendar that it would never succeed without teacher buy-in. The opportunity for greater pay and for vacation time at "off-peak" times of the year was seen as an incentive. Haser and Nasser have done a wonderful job of capturing the reaction of teachers to the modified-calendar concept in Fairfax. It is a valuable resource to others planning to implement this concept in their communities. We appreciate the time and effort they spent in gathering this information.

Dan Domenech
Senior Vice President
McGraw-Hill Education
National Urban Markets

Preface

Year-round education, also referred to as modified-calendar schooling, has increased over the past twenty years. Many districts and schools are exploring or currently implementing this model in response to student achievement in high-needs or low-performing schools, which typically have a high number of Title I, ESOL, and/or minority students. For the most part, schools have focused on the academic benefits for students on a modified calendar; however, this book highlights the benefits this year-round calendar holds for teachers.

Teacher motivation and retention are critical issues in high-needs schools, and this book explains the transition process of three schools and the resultant impact on teacher motivation through real-life case study examples. The book was also written to serve as a reference source for schools that need general information, guidance, or direction in switching from a traditional calendar to a year-round or modified calendar. In the case studies, the principals' leadership and motivation style are included and discussed as well.

The use of actual schools (which have been given pseudonyms) through a case study approach is one significant benefit of this book. Through the case study model, the authors spent over two years studying in-depth the teachers, the principals, and the transitions brought about by those parties. A feature of the book is the breakdown of case studies by chapters with practical, useful information for a wide range of professionals such as teachers, principals, superintendents, school board members, teacher education faculty, preservice teachers, professional development school partners, state departments of education employees, and school leadership or policy students who seek a transition or are interested in learning about year-round or modified-calendar schools. Also, many groups or individuals outside of education may be interested in this book such as parents, state and local legislatures, members of community advisory boards, and organization advocates for ESL/ESOL, immigrant, urban inner-city school renewal, and high-needs or at-risk students.

Acknowledgments

We would like to recognize the generous support of Fairfax County Public Schools, particularly the school principals, who enthusiastically gave us access to their schools over the course of many months: Susan Akroyd, Anita Blain, and Dr. Teresa West.

A word of praise is also owed to other school administrators and coordinators who generously supplied us with information, answered our questions, and granted us interviews, including Diane Connolly, Terry Corey, Katherine Freeman, Donna Lewis, Kathleen McDonald, David Seligsohn, and Tim Stanley.

A heartfelt thank you goes out to the dozens of teachers and specialists at Glen Forest, Parklawn, and Timber Lane Elementary Schools who met with us at odd hours of the day and gave up precious time to interview for this book. The frank and candid thoughts they offered during our conversations provided valuable insight, which made this book possible.

Many individuals at the National Association for Year-Round Education (NAYRE) were particularly helpful in sharing information and data, and we thank them as well.

Alysha Warren faithfully transcribed all of the interview tapes and prepared the index; we are grateful for her excellent work.

Shelly thanks her husband Dan for his support and encouragement during the research and writing of this book. She also salutes her mom, a constant source of encouragement.

Ilham thanks her husband and children. Without the unwavering support of her husband, Mohammed, and her beautiful children, Ayman and Luma, this project would not have been achieved. Mohammed has truly been a source of inspiration throughout the process. Ilham thanks her parents, who always believed in her and in education as a means to change minority children's lives.

CHAPTER 1

Introduction

Year-round education or modified-calendar schooling has increased dramatically in the United States and Canada in the past twenty years. This book focuses on year-round or modified calendar schools, and specifically on teachers and their job motivation, their work environment at school, and the qualities of their professional lives. Also, leadership styles of school principals are discussed as they relate to teacher motivation and the alternative school calendar. The actions of five principals who were a part of a transition from a traditional- to a year-round or modified-calendar school schedule are examined to understand their impact on the level of motivation of their teachers.

According to NAYRE, since 1980, more than 3,000 schools have transitioned from a traditional calendar to a year-round schedule. Even though the idea of students attending school throughout the year is not new, it is an idea whose time has come for many communities and schools. The benefits of a modified school year are often found to be an improvement in both academic and nonacademic outcomes among students, teachers, parents, and communities.

WHAT ARE YEAR-ROUND EDUCATION OR MODIFIED-CALENDAR SCHOOLS?

There are basically two models or designs of year-round education or modified calendar schools. A "single-track" year-round education calendar is most often used to provide a more balanced educational opportunity to students, while a multiple track or "multitrack" calendar is designed to alleviate prevailing space or overcrowding problems at a school. Under both formats, students are in school the same number of days as a traditional-calendar school with the long summer recess broken up more evenly throughout the twelve months. For example, usually there are two-week vacation breaks in October, January, and March, along with standard U.S. holidays such as Thanksgiving, winter recess or Christmas vacation, and spring break or Easter vacation. The reasons for which schools implement a single-track or multitrack calendar are usually different.

A multitrack calendar is most often implemented when schools must accommodate a large number of students in one school and/or when districts are forced to cut costs and operate fewer school facilities for a great number of students. In a multitrack calendar, students and teachers are typically divided into three or four groups or tracks with respective vacation periods staggered throughout the year. Each track has its own schedule, which means that students and teachers in one track may be on vacation while the other tracks are in school. Multitracking is seen as a way for districts to deal with overcrowded schools without building new facilities since there is always a track attending school.

Throughout North America, the single-track calendar has been more widely adopted than the multitrack calendar. In many areas of the country, single-track calendar schools are often referred to as modified-calendar schools (i.e., modified-calendar schools are generally *not* multitrack schools). In 1999, over half of the year-round schools in the United States and Canada declared a single-track or modified-calendar schedule.

Like multitrack-calendar schools, single-track or modified-calendar schools also have students and teachers attend, at minimum, the same number of days as their peers and colleagues in traditional schools located in the same district or school system. Both the multitrack and single-track schedules distribute summer vacation more evenly throughout the twelve months.

The main differences between the multitrack and single-track or modified calendar is that the multitrack must accommodate overcrowding in schools while the single-track or modified calendar focuses on reducing summer learning loss, especially with students who have limited English language ability. Also, the single-track or modified calendar offers more in-school learning days in the form of intersession courses, which is generally not the case for multitrack schools.

On the single-track or modified-calendar schedule, most schools adopt the quarter system that involves forty-five days in school followed by fifteen days of break. The school year begins in late July with two-week breaks in October, January, and March. In addition to those breaks, students also have the traditional U.S. school holidays, such as Thanksgiving, winter or Christmas vacation, and spring or Easter break, with the rest of the school system.

For at-risk and low-income students, the benefits of the single-track or modified-calendar schedule have been shown to include a reduced summer learning loss, a lessening of academic burnout, and improvement of specific skills such as English for nonnative speakers. Based on standardized test scores, schools that were unsuccessfully educating at-risk, low-income, and minority or immigrant students have found the single-track year-round or modified calendar schedule to be a good fit for the students' educational and emotional needs.

This book focuses on the single-track year-round or modified-calendar schedule. *When the term "year-round education" or "modified calendar" is used from this point forward, it implies the single-track schedule.*

According to John Ansman, principal of Roosevelt-Perry School in Jefferson County Kentucky, 95 percent of his students were eligible for Title I, which means they qualified for federally funded subsidized breakfast and lunches. The school recently switched to a year-round format since his students were losing a vast amount of knowledge and learning opportunities over the summer break (www.nayre.org).

WHY STUDY YEAR-ROUND OR MODIFIED SCHOOLING?

The majority of research on year-round or modified-calendar schools is conducted to evaluate student achievement, mostly for poor, at-risk students, and/or students with limited English ability. However, there are many other positive benefits that a year-round school schedule can have on other groups who comprise the school community. One group in particular is teachers. There has been little research conducted or dialogue undertaken to gain an understanding of teachers in year-round or modified-calendar schools, especially in relation to motivation, stress, and the school environment.

The research for this book, which primarily focuses on teacher motivation, their work environment, and the quality of their professional life, was conducted at three Title I elementary schools which transitioned from a traditional calendar to a year-round or modified calendar in order to improve academic outcomes for their predominately limited–English speaking student populations. The reason that the three schools restructured their academic year was to increase student learning time so that the students, many of whom were second language learners of English, might become better prepared in all areas of academic learning.

What the authors discovered at the three schools was a significant trend that showed highly motivated teachers whose professional satisfaction owed to a variety of reasons connected to the quality of professional life created by the modified calendar.

WHAT IS A CASE STUDY?

For years case studies have been used for teaching and learning in the fields of law and business. It has only been fairly recent, in the last ten years or so, that case studies have been systematically utilized for understanding many different areas in the field of education. A case study looks in-depth over a period of time at one particular situation in order to gain a deeper understanding of the interaction or perspectives between the people and the dilemmas or challenges they face. Case studies can provide a detailed analysis of the dynamics for a particular group. Case study readers must use higher level thinking skills by pulling apart each piece of the case study and judging or analyzing it. This is generally done through a small group discussion.

Researching for a case study must take place in the actual case study setting. The researchers must go to that setting in order to observe and interview the people. Case study data are organized into "themes" that arise from the information gained through interviews and observation notes.

For this book, the authors spent over two years at three Title I schools to understand how the calendar impacted teachers' motivation and the quality of their professional life. Methods of work for this book were designed from the case study approach, which included interviews, classroom observations, anecdotal evidence, and school records.

In all, there were forty-five recorded interviews of teachers, current and past administrators, and specialists, such as English Speakers of Other Languages (ESOL) teachers. The interviews were conducted voluntarily and designed to promote a conversation based on a set of questions. All participants knew that the conversation would be tape recorded and transcribed. The results of the interviews were then analyzed in order to discern major categories and themes relating to teacher motivation and the quality of their professional life. Also, the authors made observations of activities throughout the school facilities, not just in classrooms.

The case study approach allowed for in-depth contact at the school and with the teachers over an extended period of time. Such quantity of time gave the authors a thorough picture of the environmental factors that affect teacher motivation at a year-round or modified-calendar school at those particular schools. *It is important to note that the findings from these case studies should not be generalized as being applicable to all year-round or modified-calendar schools; however, the findings may promote further understanding or insight at other schools.*

OVERVIEW OF FAIRFAX COUNTY PUBLIC SCHOOLS

The three schools highlighted in this book are located in the FCPS system in Fairfax County, Virginia. It is a large school system in a county that spans 395 square miles. With an enrollment of 166,601 students, FCPS ranks twelfth in the county by national enrollment standards (www.fcps.edu). The county educates a diverse ethnic, racial, religious, and economic student population.

Fairfax County has a total of 136 elementary schools and implements a variety of special programs within many of those schools that target specific students. For example, in seventeen schools, some of which have significantly lower standardized test scores, there are programs such as "Success by Eight." This program includes elements such as multi-ge and looping classes, to ensure that children will master reading and do mathematics on grade level by age eight.

FCPS provide ESOL programs to 20,500 Pre-kindergarten through grade 12 students in 201 out of the 241 schools in the county. The ESOL programs include school-based instruction or centers for students in grades 1–12, who collectively speak more than one hundred languages other than English.

Since 1998, the school system has focused much attention and resources on Title I schools through the "Plan of Excellence" or EXCEL program, which was created to target the schools that have large numbers of students who are at risk for failing to master subject matters. The risk assessment is based on the scores received on standardized tests under the statewide Virginia Standards of Learning (SOL).

A student who is eligible for Title I service (Title I student) is one who lives at or below the poverty level, based on his or her parents' income. Thus designated, the student receives free or reduced-price school breakfast and lunch and additional Title I funding for appropriate instructional services such as "reading recovery." Designation as a "school-wide" Title I school means that at least 40 percent of the student population is eligible for such meals, and additional federal funds are allocated for instructional resources on a wider scale for the students.

Faculty and principals at Title I schools consult with county administrators and Title I offices to design their own plans or initiatives for utilizing Title I funds at their respective schools. The funding applications must cite research to show that the respective plan should raise achievement levels for all students. Schools may combine the federal government Title I funds and the county EXCEL funds to implement appropriate academic or achievement programs.

The county's EXCEL program schools must choose and implement a research-based extended-time model from the following choices: a year-round or modified calendar, full day Monday, or Saturday school. Also, the school must choose an instructional program from an approved list of many that includes programs such as the Literacy Collaborative from Ohio State. Also, instruction must have students incorporate technology-based phonics instruction with a ninety-minute block of uninterrupted literacy. The faculty, school administrators, and school area directors of the EXCEL schools are then given latitude in the selection of individual programs to improve their academic achievement. The overall success of Project EXCEL is measured individually by the yearly improvement in each school's county achievement index score, which is the state standardized SOL test.

Two out of the three schools examined for this book are both school-wide Title I and EXCEL schools. All three schools switched to a year-round or modified-calendar school to target student achievement on the state standardized test. By 2003, one of the schools, which had been on the modified calendar since 1998, reached its goal of academic achievement. The second school in 2004 also reached its state-approved target for academic success, and as of 2004, the third school has shown improvement based on standardized test scores. The names of the schools have been replaced with pseudonyms.

THE HEART OF YEAR-ROUND OR MODIFIED SCHEDULES: INTERSESSIONS

Intersessions are the breaks or vacation periods throughout the year, which generally apply to the single-track year-round or modified-calendar school. During those breaks, many schools conduct an intersession program that offers a variety of academic, cultural, athletic, remedial, and artistic opportunities for the students. Such programs take various forms but are often simply referred to as an intersession. The intersession program is generally not mandatory for students, but in many Title I schools it is highly promoted and structured to appeal to both the students' interests and needs.

The strength of the single-track calendar is the intersession program: correspondingly, a multitrack schedule may have more difficulty with incorporating such a program because classroom and other space is a commodity in short supply. Not withstanding that, some multitrack schools have developed the flexibility and creativity to successfully conduct intersession programs.

Often Title I schools, which tend to educate many low-income or second language learners of English, switch to a year-round or modified calendar to allow students more time in school—up to thirty more school days through intersession classes. This means that the intersession program classes are vitally important to the fundamental mission of providing more in-school learning time for students.

Students who do choose to attend the intersession(s) in Fairfax County Public Schools generally pay a fee of $25.00 per intersession, and assistance is available for students who cannot pay this fee. Students may select the topic or unit that they will learn about over that two-week period. An intersession class typically last four hours per day and are generally divided into morning and afternoon sessions. Students may attend both sessions, and thus spend an eight-hour day at school.

Intersession offerings are diverse, ranging from academic topics with a remedial focus, such as "Math Magic" or "Science Surprise," to acquiring new skills and hobbies, such as gardening, photography, and sports. A review of records at one school revealed that a high percentage of students, about 85 percent, participate in one or more of the intersession classes. *As a result, most of the students spend more days at school each year than their peers at non–year round or modified-calendar schools.*

Intersession instructors or teachers are not necessarily the teachers who make up the regular faculty at a school. The year-round or modified-calendar schools in many districts attract intersession teachers from a vast pool of human resources, including retired teachers, teachers on family leave or those staying home with their children, university graduate students, university professors, retired military personnel, and retired or part-time business professionals, such as photographers or bakers.

In most year-round or modified-calendar schools, teachers are not required to work during the intersessions and thus work the same contract days as their colleagues at traditional-calendar schools. Also, if teachers at the year-round or modified-calendar school want to teach an intersession class, they receive pay for that service, which is in addition to their regular salary.

The Intersession Coordinator

In many schools there is an intersession coordinator who is a full-time employee with the responsibility for planning and running the intersession classes, evaluating instructors, and assessing student outcomes. Frequently, the intersession coordinator is a former teacher at the school who also has or is working toward school administration credentials or certification. In Fairfax County, this position is often a steppingstone to becoming an assistant principal. In other school systems, several teachers work as a team to fulfill the role of the intersession coordinator, and each earns a stipend.

In nearly all schools, the intersession coordinator has many administrative responsibilities during the breaks, since the intersessions are typically held during the time when principals and assistant principals take leave. For that reason, many intersession coordinators find that the intersessions offer a fulfilling opportunity for them to both demonstrate and enhance their administrative skills.

The coordinator must be able to evaluate the intersession lesson plans and units of study in order for them to extend or meet the curriculum learning outcome requirements set by the state or county. The intersession coordinator is viewed as serving a vital role in extending the curriculum to meet the needs of the students. Many schools decide to implement a year-round or modified calendar because of the extended learning time and attendant educational value afforded by the intersession classes. At most schools, for all intents and purposes, the intersession classes amount to *the* reason for the school to be on a modified calendar.

A LOOK AT THE LITERATURE

In 2003, most public schools in the United Sates operated on a school calendar for reasons of the prevailing tradition and resistance to change the status quo. In the late 1800s and early 1900s, a much larger segment of the population worked in agricultural-related jobs, and children and teenagers were an important workforce on many family farms (Glines and Bingle, 2002). Often schools were in session based on the needs of the farming community, which likely meant that schools closed during the summer and early fall months. During that time, many schools in the hot, humid areas of the south and east were also closed during the summer since schools did not have air conditioning.

Today, the traditional reasons (farming and lack of air conditioning) for operating a nine-month school calendar are, for the most part, irrelevant. The September to June format of schooling is so entrenched in U.S. public school systems and in family life that it is difficult for many to objectively consider the reasons for operating a continuous or twelve-month calendar school. Given this tradition and resistance to change, some of the outcomes of the nine-month calendar have not been critically examined, particularly in areas where children and youth are without regular adult supervision, without stimulating and safe recreation areas, and without English language exposure and learning opportunities. The loss of language and academic skills over the summer months often requires weeks of review when school resumes, thus, greater loss of instructional time (Cohen, Cordi, Kitchen, and Ryan, 2000).

Many schools around the world have always operated on closer to a year-round basis than the September to June U.S. model. For example, public schools in England, Switzerland, Germany, and Russia have up to 220 school days with breaks in October, December/January, February, and July. Japan and other Asian countries have a 240-day school year with time off throughout twelve months. The foreign perspective often holds that the idea of the long summer school break in the United States lends itself almost entirely to recreation and socialization, and not academics.

Year-round education in the United States is not a new concept; the first year-round education school opened its doors in Indiana in 1904 (Glines, 1995). According to the year-round education model, students attend school for the whole year or twelve months with breaks scheduled throughout the academic year. Many schools switched to this alternative calendar mainly to solve problems such as low achievement scores amongst at-risk students and overcrowding in schools. Contrary to the public misconception, the major goal of the model is not only to increase the number of schooling days beyond 180 but to increase instructional contact time by spreading out the school session differently than the traditional school calendar (Palmer and Bernis, 1999).

Many school districts choose the year-round or modified model with the belief that this will shorten achievement gaps and improve students' standardized test scores. There are many schools and districts that are finding the year-round or modified calendar is successful in meeting their academic goals, even though there continues to be widespread public rejection of and skepticism toward the model as well as mixed research results when it comes to student achievement in non–high needs schools.

However, the year-round calendar has shown many positive outcomes in relation to academic achievement with at-risk or high-needs students and students who are learning English as a second language (Davies and Trevor, 1999). Several studies on the year-round calendar, which were conducted in major school districts, revealed that it is beneficial for students in improving attendance and academic achievement, as well as reducing discipline problems (Ballinger, 2000; Barber, 1996; Warrick-Harris, 1995).

When comparing year-round and traditional school models, the evidence that at-risk students have benefited academically from an alternative calendar model is overwhelming (Campbell, 1994; Capps and Cox, 1991; Gandara and Fish, 1994; Kneese, 1996; Shields and Oberg, 1999). In many cases where students were offered remedial education classes during the breaks or intersessions, accompanied by curriculum changes in programs, the year-round format proved to be essential for at-risk students (Shields and LaRocque, 1998).

School districts that choose the year-round education model generally examine the advantages and disadvantages that the alternative calendar would bring to students and their families. Despite the reports on the benefits this modified calendar has for students, there is still widespread public resistance to the idea. The National Association for Year-Round Education (NAYRE) explained that those persons who have the most difficulty accepting the change are teachers and parents. They simply cannot let go of their routine.

Studies on nonacademic aspects of year-round education suggested that students in general are more motivated and ready to learn (Davies and Trevor, 1999). Furthermore, parents and students enjoyed the freedom of school choice often found where this model is offered (Barber, 1996; Campbell, 1994).

Teacher Motivation and the Modified School Calendar

Teacher quality and teacher retention have commanded much media attention, especially in rural and urban schools and areas with large numbers of poor, minority, and limited-English-proficient students (Southward, 2000). In addition, Southward's findings reported that 30–50 percent of all new teachers will leave the profession within the first five years for a variety of reasons. Professional stress and burnout were cited in different studies as being an influence in teachers' decision to leave the profession.

Teacher retention factors must be addressed if quality teachers are to stay in the profession through retirement age. Teacher motivation may be one key to understanding the reasons for which teachers leave the profession and pursue other opportunities outside of education (Frase, 1993). Policy makers, school administrators, and district superintendents, as well as the public, may benefit from an understanding of the link between teacher retention and teacher motivation.

Several studies examined intrinsic and extrinsic sources of motivation in relation to job satisfaction. Ellis (1984) noted that external rewards such as salaries and bonus packages are the benefits involved with the job. Intrinsic rewards include the emotional and personal benefits of the job such as professional growth and a sense of accomplishment. Ellis claims that intrinsic rewards play a more critical role in job satisfaction among teachers. Intrinsic motivation can be improved through job enrichment practices such as professional development options (Luce, 1998). Research findings connected to teacher motivation reported that teachers were happier and motivated to teach when both intrinsic and extrinsic factors were met (Feistritzer, 1986; Frase, 1993).

It is important here to examine how the modified calendar might impact teacher motivation by using Frederick Herzberg's (1966) classical theory of motivation and "hygienes," which was applied to teacher motivation by more recent researchers such as Haser and Nasser (2003). Herzberg originally looked at factors that lead accountants and engineers to be satisfied or motivated at their job, which was often tied to the physical and emotional work environment.

Herzberg found that employee achievement, recognition (for achievement), advancement or promotion, responsibility, and the nature of the job itself (challenging and interesting) are all major intrinsic motivators for an individual to want to do well at work. He also emphasized the importance of another set of factors, which he called "hygiene." Those factors include interpersonal relations with colleagues, peers, and supervisors, along with the work policies, administration layout (e.g., top to bottom environment), working conditions, and personal life outside of the office. When those factors are not gratified, an individual will create negative attitudes, producing dissatisfaction with work. Consequently, the motivating factors combine to relate more to job satisfaction than dissatisfaction while the "hygiene" factors contribute more to the opposite, job dissatisfaction than to job satisfaction.

Herzberg's research suggested that individuals were positive and satisfied at work when there were many motivational practices present, such as getting recognition for achievement (e.g., employee of the month, spotlight on faculty, etc.) and when challenging and interesting responsibilities were involved. On the other hand, workers felt negatively or dissatisfied at their job when there were unpleasant interpersonal relationships with supervisors, colleagues, and/or there were administration practices and/or policies that were demeaning or unreasonable (e.g., teachers signing in at the office every morning).

Haser and Nasser (2003) applied Herzberg's theory to the year-round or modified calendar and found that it led teachers to be more satisfied or motivated at their job for several reasons. In relation to a motivating factor identified as "work itself," teachers expressed more enjoyment in teaching when there were frequent breaks throughout the twelve months or when there was an opportunity to instruct an intersession class based on the teachers' interest or talent. The breaks spread out over the year also contributed to satisfaction with the "hygiene" factors of "working conditions" and "interpersonal relations with peers" due to co-teaching and team-teaching opportunities found in the intersession classes. Nasser and Haser (2002) also found that when teachers were an instrumental piece of changing a traditional school to a year-round or modified-calendar model, they were inspired to teach because many "hygiene" and motivating factors, such as "interpersonal relations with peers and administrators," "achievement," and "recognition" were satisfied.

Other research findings related to teacher job satisfaction and year-round or modified-calendar schools found that teachers and administrators reported positive attitudes in school social climate, increased faculty communication, innovations in teaching and learning, and less teacher stress or burnout (Campbell, 1994; Gandara, 1992; Shields and LaRocque 1998; Shields and Oberg, 1999).

The issue of reducing teacher stress is an important one to examine because teachers who work in high-needs schools report higher levels of stress and burnout. Keeping teachers' stress levels to a minimum may help to sustain motivation (Czubai, 1996). According to Parkaway, Olejnik, and Proller (1988), teachers in low-stress schools developed ". . . less physical symptoms of job-related stress and fewer psychological/emotional stress symptoms" (20).

In addition, it has been suggested that teachers who were stressed influenced their students' stress level. Also, those teachers who had a low self-regard became burned out (Czubai, 1996). However, there is a link between job satisfaction and professional stress level. Job satisfaction not only motivates people to remain in a job despite higher levels of stress, but also to become better teachers (Smith and Bourke, 1990).

There seems to be agreement that the year-round or modified-calendar model offers a reduction in stress level and an increase in motivation among teachers. There is also evidence that in the case of the single-track calendar there was a decrease in teachers' absenteeism (Kocek, 1996).

There is also a strong suggestion that teachers' attitudes toward the year-round calendar improve when they try it (Loyd, 1991). The attitudes measured in Loyd's study pertained to year-round education, scheduling, and school quality. In another study where teachers were asked about the ease of scheduling around their personal lives and family activities, teachers in year-round education schools expressed more satisfaction than teachers on the traditional calendar (Elsberry, 1992).

Models of Leadership

There is a vast difference between a principal who is perceived as simply an administrator and one who is a leader. Administrators focus on stability and efficiency, while leaders tend to stress adaptive change and getting individuals to agree on what action the group or organization needs to take and then motivating them to accomplish the work (Hoy and Miskel, 1996). Leaders are more visionary and inspirational with people, whereas administrators are more apt to organize, control, and solve problems (Kotter, 1990). Others feel that leadership effectiveness is contingent upon matching leadership style with an appropriate situation.

There is not a clear-cut definition of effective leaders and administrators. However, there are numerous leadership theories that identify the qualities of a leader and the motivational styles that make them successful at their jobs.

Principals in year-round or modified-calendar schools must be somewhat innovative or be part of a team that is so, since an alternative calendar model is generally not the norm in most areas of the United States. Many principals who find themselves in the process of leading a school to a year-round calendar may be exhibiting traits that are considered to be those of a transformational leader (Bass, 1985), transactional leader, and/or a leader who subscribes to goal setting.

Transformational Leadership

According to Hoy and Miskel, "Transformational leaders are expected to define the need for change, create new visions, concentrate on long-term goals, inspire followers to transcend their own interests for higher order goals, change the organization to accommodate their vision rather than work within the existing one, mentor followers to take greater responsibility for their own development, and [ensure] that followers become leaders and leaders become change agents" (393).

Also, transformational leaders are highly creative, admired, respected, and trusted, and followers want to emulate them. Their motivational strategy tends to be "inspirational motivation" (Atwater and Bass, 1994), which creates a sense of team spirit, enthusiasm, optimism, goal commitment, and a group approach to formulating a shared vision.

Transactional Leadership

Transactional leadership (Burns, 1978) is a style that incorporates some transformational leadership traits and motivating aspects. Politicians often use this style by exchanging rewards for services, such as lower taxes for votes: if you vote for me, I'll lower your taxes. Parents also use this tactic frequently with children, and it is often referred to as "Grandma's rules": if you eat your vegetables you can go outside and play. Transactional principals give teachers and staff members what they want in exchange for things the principal wants. A good example is for a principal to want higher test scores and teachers who want more instructional support for the students. Transactional leading can be effective and motivating with teachers, if aligned with the right individuals who respond to this approach.

Goal Setting

Goal setting is a pragmatic, popular motivational style that simply states that when an individual or group is committed to a goal and wants to accomplish it (Locke and Lantham, 1990), the goal will be achieved. Goal setting has been shown to have positive effects on motivation and job performance, especially when individuals are aware of and help to set the individual and group goals. It is not a creative, dynamic approach, but it is efficient when used in the appropriate setting. This style features a traditional top-down approach and often allows for little creativity or leeway.

Authoritarian

The least effective is one of the oldest styles of leading, which is an authoritarian structure (Hall, 1962). This style emphasizes power in relation to position and hierarchy. Power is centered at the top and flows downward. The superior always has the last word. In a school or environment where group consensus, input, and visionary change is needed, this style is the least compatible and least successful. Generally speaking, the group, school, or principal operating under the authoritarian style will fail to achieve long-reaching visionary goals, such as transitioning to a year-round or modified-calendar schedule.

SUMMARY

Year-round education is not a new concept. However, many schools and school systems in the past twenty years have had a renewed interest in this calendar for a variety of reasons. Schools that implemented a year-round or modified calendar found the intersession classes was a key piece since students may spend up to thirty more days in school for instruction than their peers. The intersession coordinator was a vital person as she or he must be certain that, along with other responsibilities, intersession classes align with curriculum standards and are outcome-based.

The following three case studies are year-round or modified-calendar schools in the Fairfax County Public Schools, the twelfth largest school system in the county. The schools switched to a modified calendar in order to meet the needs of the students who were limited English speaking and not meeting the state and county goals for standardized tests. However, what was also learned was that the modified calendar has many benefits for teachers as well. Teachers tend to be more motivated at their job on this calendar.

The research on motivation implied that intrinsic motivation was much more gratifying and powerful than extrinsic factors. The modified calendar provided many intrinsic motivational factors for teachers that are further discussed in the following case studies. School leadership styles were also reviewed, and those styles are expanded upon in the following case studies as well.

CHAPTER 2

First Case Study:
Green Meadow Elementary School

SCHOOL DESCRIPTION AND POPULATION

Green Meadow Elementary School (pseudonym) was built in 1955 and was recently renovated. Over the past forty-seven years, the school has grown to serve a diverse community. This Title I school had a student population comprised from over sixty countries with a recent enrollment of 572 students. The school was Fairfax County's first school to operate on a year-round or modified calendar.

Students at the school enjoyed the benefits of a renovated building, which included a large library, larger classrooms, and a more aesthetically pleasing environment. Also, a wireless mobile computer lab afforded the opportunity to learn through cutting-edge technology practices. As expressed on the school's 2004 website, staff and community members believed that six principles guided their actions as professionals:

> All children can and will learn. Ethnicity, cultural and religious backgrounds, family education, income level, or conditions in the home do not affect the ability of the child to learn; nor will such factors decrease the exemplary effort given in teaching the students. Parents want and deserve the best education for their children and they deserve full support in coeducating their child or children.

This chapter is focused on the process by which this school switched from a traditional to a modified calendar, the principals' leadership styles as part of that process, and the resultant effect on teacher motivation under the new modified calendar. Green Meadow teachers were feeling frustrated in the mid-1990s by their lack of time for planning and reflection; they were truly interested in changing the instructional format of the school day and year in order to benefit the predominately minority, at-risk students at this school. The major frustration they voiced was the lack of sufficient instructional time to meet the needs of their students. So the teachers embarked on a plan for change. By 1998, the teachers had successfully spearheaded a three-year transition from the traditional calendar to a modified-calendar school through the support and guidance of the school and county administrators.

This was the first year-round or modified-calendar school in the county, and it eventually paved the way for six other county elementary schools with similar student populations to move to a modified calendar.

LESSONS LEARNED AT GREEN MEADOW

Green Meadow had been functioning on a modified calendar for three years when the work for this case study started. During the interviews (see a list of questions in appendix B), teachers and specialists reflected and talked in great length about the transition process from a traditional calendar to a year-round or modified-calendar school, and the impact of the new calendar, which they felt enhanced the quality of their teaching or "job performance" and motivated them to want to teach in this high-needs school. Part of the former and current school administrators' discussions included their roles in the transition and post-transition years.

The following themes emerged from the discussions and observations at Green Meadow:

1. Teachers felt empowered through ownership of the transition process from a traditional to a modified-calendar school.
2. Teachers felt supported by their colleagues, school administrators, and county administrators for their work in changing to a modified calendar and in their teaching endeavors after the switch.
3. The calendar assisted in reducing professional stress and burnout and presented teachers with professional options not necessarily available in traditional-calendar schools.

4. The school administrators' leadership style was a key factor in the teachers' motivation before, during, and after the transition from a traditional to a modified-calendar school.
5. The alternative calendar presented a few obstacles.

FIRST THEME: TEACHER EMPOWERMENT OF THE PROCESS

The uniqueness of the transition in this school stems from the fact that teachers felt they had ownership over the process from a traditional to a year-round or modified-calendar school. This ownership seemed to play an important role in motivating teachers. In a preceding discussion, support from colleagues and superiors was cited as a factor for greater teacher motivation. Support alone and in and of itself may not be sufficient to motivate teachers without the empowerment that teachers said they needed. One of the best examples is that the whole idea to examine a year-round or modified calendar as a new school schedule actually came from a group of Green Meadow teachers—it was their initial idea!

Teachers' Involvement in the Decision-Making Process

Green Meadow teachers took the lead in learning about year-round or modified-calendar schooling. They exerted much effort in attending conferences, visiting other schools, and gathering information about the model. Eventually the *teachers* came to the conclusion that this schedule was best for the majority of students. The teachers viewed themselves as an integral part of the decision-making process and implementation.

One teacher commented, "Our student body [has] mostly working parents with more than two jobs and they work all week. Not only does it [the calendar] give the children more time in school [via the intersessions] . . . they are in school rather than on the streets or just sitting in front of a television."

The previous principal who facilitated the teachers in the process noted that "The teachers had a common problem of how to teach such a large curriculum in just 180 days. They usually managed somehow but always complained about the fact that they don't have enough time. This was the beginning of a three-year self-examination process where *teachers* looked at the transition as a good possibility."

At the very beginning of the whole process, the principal told the teachers who complained about curriculum fragmentation due to scheduling: "Lets form a committee. . . . I am willing to hear your suggestions on how to deal with that." Eighteen enthusiastic teachers jumped at the opportunity. According to the teachers who took part in the transition, many of whom were veteran teachers, they formed a think tank open to all teachers. Members of the think tank brought ideas on how to increase learning time in a student-centered environment. In addition to a modified calendar, they also explored lengthening the school day or offering more summer school courses.

One of the teachers noticed an invitation to a conference on year-round education and brought the idea up at a meeting. Shortly thereafter, two teachers traveled to the conference to learn more about the idea and to check whether it might be a good model for their school. The teachers were excited about the information presented at the conference and shared the knowledge gained with the think tank. The group then decided to pursue changing from a traditional calendar into a year-round or modified-calendar school.

The succeeding principal, who had served as one of the teachers on the think tank committee, recalled: "There was a general excitement that this might be a solution to have more instructional time on hand but there was also skepticism that the county would not allow us to do so because of the cost and conflicting schedules."

Despite frustrations experienced at some junctures during the first years of the process, the committee kept studying the proposal while the [former] principal was communicating the teachers' findings to county administrators.

In the second year when teachers were convinced that they wanted to move on with the transition, they solicited input from the community. The principal immediately formed a steering committee made up of interested parents. The principal even took two parents and three more teachers to the next year-round education annual conference to learn more about intersessions and the whole idea of extended learning time. Meanwhile, teachers led community meetings and answered parents' questions. Teachers also listened to concerns and tried to respond to those parents who opposed the idea.

After a series of meetings were held, the community voted in overwhelming support of the transition, which allowed the teachers and administrators to move forward with the plan. According to the assistant principal, 87 percent of the school community voted in favor of the idea, which was a great success for the teachers.

The teachers revealed that they were all ready to transition to the new calendar by the end of the second year, but school board members and the superintendent, Dr. Daniel Domenech, requested that they wait a third year in order to work out all the details. The third year of preparation proved to be worthwhile as the principal and assistant principal worked out many details and logistics with the county, such as transportation, food services, and special education services.

SECOND THEME: SUPPORT OF TEACHING ENDEAVORS

There were three levels of support that teachers felt were important to their efforts as they moved towards a year-round or modified calendar. Those levels were: the support from the county, the support from the school administration, and lastly, the support of fellow school colleagues who all shared the school's vision and mission revolving around the students and the modified calendar. The authors opine that each of those sources of support motivated teachers in their jobs, especially during the transition period.

County-Level Support

The support the teachers received started at a higher level within the school system's hierarchy, specifically with their area director or "cluster director." The cluster director's responsibility was to oversee the principals and academic progress of the schools in a specific part of the county. The cluster director's support provided teachers with professional respect and confidence in pursuing the modified calendar option. Teachers articulated that the county-level administrators listened to their ideas and concerns (through a small group of teacher representatives and school administrators) and worked with them, the teachers.

Teachers knew they had the option to look into a change in the instructional format in their school, which would include more time in school for students. At the beginning of the process, one teacher described how several teachers examined a handful of instructional models that allowed more learning time with children.

She said, "A few teachers read about year-round education and became interested in learning more about it. They went to the principal and asked her if they could attend a conference. The principal approved the idea and covered the cost of it."

The cluster director helped to obtain the school board's approval of the transition as a whole. The transition required additional budgets; in this case it was about $250,000 in additional cost for staffing, transportation, and intersessions. This was costly, but the county was willing to invest in the school. In addition to cost, the cluster director also assisted in working out many details and schedules relating to food services, custodians, office staff, staffing intersessions, and special education services, etc. Without the support of the county, those important details would not have been worked out as smoothly, or possibly at all, as the previous principal recounted in her interview.

The cluster director and other higher-level county administrators played an important role in securing the county school board's approval to expand the services of additional professionals at Green Meadow once it changed to a modified calendar. Those resources and services included a psychologist, social worker, resource teachers, and a parent liaison (Spanish speaking), who helped communicate with and meet the needs of the diverse community that was predominately Hispanic.

Principal's Support

It was clear that the county-level support would not have been won were it not for the school administrator's leadership in facilitating the process. The school principal served as a liaison to the county and as an advocate for the teachers. Teachers felt that school-wide support was provided from both the school administrators and from their own colleagues on the faculty.

The former principal's leadership was described by one of the teachers who said that "the policy of most administrators in this school is to have the staff be part of the decision making process . . . then you [the teacher] buy into it and are more supportive of it."

The teachers felt that if they were involved as an integral part of the decision-making process, no matter what the issue, they were more likely to cooperate and act upon decisions made by the group. Transitioning to a different school calendar was a major change, and without the leadership of the school administration through their cooperative approach, teachers would have most likely resented the idea and fought it. At Green Meadow, many teachers stated that the school principal and assistant principal listened to concerns and worked toward win–win solutions. These interactions helped to develop a trusting relationship between teachers and school administrators. One teacher mentioned: "Our principal lets us do our job, and we have ownership in teaching the students."

Another example given by teachers to illustrate the cooperative approach taken by the school administration was that breaks or intersession time was structured to allow teachers to plan for the following quarter. Actually, this was a secondary reason behind transitioning to a modified calendar according to the school principal who said: "The idea [for a modified-calendar school] was also to give teachers more think time. If teachers in a specific grade level agree to meet together for a block of time during intersessions, they received a stipend for curriculum planning and reflection."

In fact, concurring sentiments were expressed by several teachers who cited a need to sometimes "step back" from the classroom, which usually happens just around the intersession or school quarter breaks. One teacher put it this way: "I have time during intersessions to just reflect about rearranging my classroom and tweaking classroom management. I come in and do all of this and get paid for it."

One teacher described the shared vision with the principal and assistant principal as "the number-one interest is children and children being successful." A veteran teacher stated, "I really like the way teachers and teams collaborate. They seem to have a vision and a goal and to know their kids and what they need. Kids come first, definitely."

In fact, all of the teachers who were interviewed expressed their agreement on the statement that their school serves children first and that the principal and assistant principal played an important role in spreading that vision among the staff and students. The administrators were described as role models for their teachers. One teacher provided this description of the atmosphere:

> The administrators here, they just don't sit in their offices doing other stuff. They are very visible. I mean the principal and assistant principal pop in here [the classroom] all the time, which is fine. They try very hard to get to know the names of all of the children in the school. They have lunch duty. You see them at bus duty. So they are really active players in the whole thing.

Colleagues' Support and Shared Vision

The supportive leadership style of the school principal and assistant principal before, during, and after the school changed to a modified calendar had a positive impact on the interactions among the faculty and staff. Several teachers described the teamwork and collaboration that existed among teachers. One teacher described the support provided by fellow faculty members: "Some schools . . . [where] I've taught . . . people tend to go in, shut their doors, and do things, and then they come back out and there is very little communication that goes on amongst the staff. In this school, that doesn't happen. Everybody is willing to share." Green Meadow teachers remained focused on their mission and collaborated to achieve that level of communication. Enormous amounts of energy were exerted daily by teachers to ensure student learning and a child-centered learning environment. Teachers expressed concerns for the population they served and whether the students were getting adequate instructional time. It was evident through the observations that school schedules, lessons, activities, and intersession courses were derived from the students' needs and interests.

The change in this school's calendar contributed to creating an atmosphere where teachers felt professionally supported by the county and school administration, as well as by fellow Green Meadow teachers. The three-tiered support system motivated teachers to believe in their ability to impact their work conditions, which eventually lead to a school environment that included extra planning time, something not found under the traditional calendar.

THIRD THEME: PROFESSIONAL OPTIONS

Most teachers at schools that operate on traditional calendars feel they have few professional options. However, many Green Meadow teachers had previously worked in schools that operated under the traditional calendar and were thereby able to compare that system with the year-round or modified calendar. Many Green Meadow teachers commented that the intersessions created more professional choices and flexibility, which increased their satisfaction in their chosen profession.

Teachers viewed the new schedule as an improvement in their work conditions, since they had frequent two-week breaks throughout twelve months. These scheduled breaks seemed to decrease teachers' feelings of professional stress and burnout. The assistant principal noted that the school data on teacher absenteeism showed that that had decreased on the modified calendar, which meant fewer substitute teachers were needed, and therefore, less money was spent. Also, the option of instructing an intersession class provided Green Meadow teachers with several professional choices that in turn dramatically enhanced their motivation or drive to continue to teach.

Intersessions and the Year-Round or Modified Calendar

Professionally, the intersessions provided four primary options for teachers, which were:

- A change from teaching the same academic subject(s) and/or the same grade level
- An opportunity to earn extra money
- Additional professional reflection and curriculum planning time
- Nontraditional periodic breaks or vacation time away from the school

Green Meadow teachers who chose to teach during the intersessions did so because they enjoyed working with other students from different grades, or they liked teaching other subjects or hobbies, and last but not least, they liked earning extra pay. Even though many intersession classes focused on remediation or academics under the county curriculum, there were curriculum extension or enrichment classes offered as well. For example, several teachers who were fluent in a foreign language used the intersession time to teach children Spanish or Chinese. Some teachers taught cooking classes, geography, and visual arts. Others focused on technology and physical education. All of the intersession classes were based on the county's Program of Study (POS) and the Virginia Standards of Learning (SOL). Each intersession class had a unit outline, lesson plans, and assessments.

The opportunity to teach during intersessions gave Green Meadow teachers on maternity or family leave a chance to keep their hand in the profession. As the assistant principal stated: "We always try something once . . . we try to be flexible. There were two teachers on maternity leave who were interested in teaching during the intersession, and arrangements were made for them to share an intersession class and keep in the [teaching] loop."

Numerous teachers continually chose to teach an intersession class and earn extra money, but those who chose not to work during the intersessions cited the opportunity to relax and rejuvenate away from school. Teachers took advantage of the nontraditional breaks by taking a cruise in October or a long ski holiday in January, both of which were not feasible under a traditional school calendar. One teacher said: "On this [modified] calendar I can take my mom to Italy in October, something I've never been able to do before."

The break during intersession also provided those teachers who had decided not to teach an opportunity to read professional journals or books and to attend workshops and conferences. One teacher mentioned the fact that she had the time to "catch up on professional reading or even attend some professional development workshops."

Several teachers talked about using the break or intersession time for planning—an advantage that was provided every nine weeks through the modified-calendar schedule. This was not usually possible when Green Meadow was functioning on a traditional school calendar. Other teachers, as mentioned earlier in the chapter, took advantage of the opportunity to teach other grade levels or to come into school during the intersession break to plan for the next quarter, for which they were paid.

The school administrators hoped that all of those professional options and opportunities offered by the modified calendar would keep the teachers refreshed, stimulated, and excited about teaching.

Intersession Breaks and Professional Stress

According to Cohen, et al. (2000), teachers on a traditional calendar feel stressed and get burned out more quickly during the lengthy traditional school year. This trend has been especially noticed in Title I schools, where teachers work with diverse children in quite demanding environments. At Green Meadow, there was a significant discussion by teachers on the decrease in professional stress because of the available breaks staggered throughout twelve months. One teacher commented:

> On the traditional calendar, I was wiped out by April. To do a good job as a teacher [in a high-needs school] took a lot out of me; I even thought of early retirement. Now, on the year-round education cycle, I get systematic breaks, the kids get breaks from me, and we're ready to work together again.

In fact, the school administration noticed that this model decreased teacher absenteeism. The assistant principal explained:

> Because they [teachers] get frequent breaks, teachers don't need to take off as many mental health days. Also teachers try to schedule their doctor's appointments during intersessions, so they don't have to take leave, which comes back around to the kids' benefit. If teachers take fewer days off, they're in the classroom more, and more learning is most likely going on than with a substitute.

The assistant principal explained that this model played an important role in reducing teachers' stress levels because it also reduced children's feelings of stress as well. The school had less discipline referrals or problems because of the schedule. In return, the fewer discipline problems helped reduce school-wide frustration that was a likely cause of stress to teachers who constantly dealt with discipline issues. The fact that both teachers and children have breaks from each other may be one reason for the more relaxed and productive school environment.

Stress and burnout are major reasons why teachers leave the profession. But at Green Meadow, teacher retention was found to be very high. Few teachers left the school unless they had newborns or had to relocate because of their spouse's job. At a time when many high-needs schools in the Washington, D.C., metropolitan area experienced shortages and fewer teaching applicants, the principal displayed a stack of applications from teachers interested in employment at the school.

FOURTH THEME: SCHOOL ADMINISTRATORS' LEADERSHIP STYLE

At Green Meadow school there were three important school administrators who displayed effective leadership styles, which was important in understanding the success of this school's transition and post-transition functioning as a modified calendar. The first principal oversaw the three years leading up to the school calendar switch and then accepted a position as a county administrator. The second principal, a former Green Meadow teacher and think tank committee member, started after the school completed its first year on the modified calendar, and as of 2004 she was still principal of the school. Throughout the whole process and as of 2004, the assistant principal remained in that position.

The principal who led the school over the three years prior to and during the first year after the transition was a successful and effective leader who displayed many aspects of *transformational leadership* (Bass, 1985), and through her inspirational motivational style (Atwater and Bass, 1994) supported the teachers' lead on exploring alternative methods for extending students' time in school.

The former principal exhibited many attractive personality traits such as being self-confident, stress-tolerant, creative, achievement-oriented, inspirational, optimistic, and highly energetic. Also, adding to the successful leadership were practices such as a *shared vision* with the group, building relationships with teachers and the community,

motivating teachers to pursue their goal, and communicating effectively with many groups of people (the superintendent's office, school
board members, county administrators, parents, and teachers). During
the process her role was that of a facilitator of the teachers' desires.
She took the lead from the teachers and utilized her communication
skills and knowledge to lead the group in the direction they wanted to
go.

The second principal continued to lead the faculty by implementing
an inspirational motivational style, something that was modeled by the
prior principal when she was a teacher and instrumental think tank
member. Although she shared many of the personality traits of the first
principal, the second principal could be described as being more subtle
and quietly diplomatic. The leadership styles of the first and second
principals complemented each other and led to the smooth and successful transition of the office of the principal.

FIFTH THEME: A FEW OBSTACLES

Since Green Meadow was the first school in the county to adopt the
year-round or modified calendar, there were a few noteworthy obstacles that the school faced during the transition and beyond. The first
obstacle was the logistical challenge in the daily operation of the
school. For example, the food service vendor had to be contacted to put
together a separate menu for the school during the summer and during
intersessions. Transportation was also an issue to be resolved because
students attended school on a different schedule and on different days
than the traditional schools in the county, and janitors and office staff
had to work more days during the twelve months.

Another challenge that the school had to work through as a pilot
school was the negative media attention it received during the transition
period. Despite the fact that about 95 percent of the parent community
backed the decision to switch calendars, the 5 percent who did not support the decision received a great deal of media attention. This action
put considerable pressure on the principal and the teachers.

One vocal parent took the issue to the media and tried to overturn
the plan through the school board. Surprisingly, this parent was granted

many press interviews and drew much attention for a few months. Eventually, the principal was able to quiet down the strong response of this one parent by offering the parents and students an excellent alternative. Those parents who stood in opposition could enroll their children at a nearby traditional-calendar school if they did not want to go to Green Meadow. Approximately twenty families accepted the offer and enrolled at the traditional-calendar school. This offer was effective for two years.

One disadvantage that has been cited by others in the field of a year-round or modified-calendar schedule relates to school administrator burnout since the school is operating thirty more days than a traditional-calendar school. The second principal explained her strategies to reduce her stress and workload. Her advice was "learn to let go," which meant that the principal should be assertive about due leave time during the year and allow the intersession coordinator to be the school administrator during the intersession breaks. The assistant principal was on a teacher's contract and was off during those breaks. The principal also mentioned that the modified calendar led to office staff burnout, and she worked to find temporary help while they took time off during the intersession breaks.

Other concerns that needed to be resolved dealt with special education, particularly pauses in individual education plans (IEPs) for school specialists such as special education teachers and therapists. Those teachers and specialists continued to follow the county's deadlines, which were aligned with a traditional school calendar. Teachers and specialists worked over their breaks or intersessions to prepare the federal mandatory Individual Education Plan (IEP) documents and other reports. The school principal paid those teachers extra money for their service and was negotiating with the county for a more permanent resolution to this important challenge.

REFLECTIONS

In this chapter, several important factors that contributed to increased teacher motivation at Green Meadow were explored. It was refreshing and optimistic to hear from teachers that they felt supported by the school and county administration for their forward thinking and hard work as teachers. Also, the modified calendar presented teachers with professional options, such as earning extra money and teaching a skill or hobby during intersession classes, which are not necessarily available in traditional-calendar schools. Teachers who chose not to instruct during intersessions found the two-week breaks every nine weeks to be rejuvenating and that they eliminated much professional stress and burnout, which helped them to focus on their high-needs students.

The administrators' transformational leadership (Bass, 1985) and inspirational motivational style (Atwater and Bass, 1994) were important elements in empowering teachers to take their idea of exploring extended learning time for students and eventually making it a reality through the modified-calendar school.

These findings from Green Meadow support the research on the importance of the work environment for increasing teachers' motivation. This positive work environment was largely influenced by the changes in the school calendar and the professional benefits it brought to teachers. The transition was motivated by the teachers' desire to service students. However, the new calendar turned out to be important for teachers as well. As many teachers said, "Once you're on this calendar you can't go back to the traditional calendar. It would be too stressful and difficult."

The length of the transition (three years) apparently was good for the teachers and school administrators as it gave time for the group to focus and research the issue in depth by attending conferences, reading research materials, and conducting their own survey among their faculty to see how willing and ready they were for this transition.

Most publications on the year-round or modified calendar state that people, especially teachers and parents, refuse to change because of the "tradition" of a September to June school year. Most families and schools have a hard time seeing past the "tradition" regardless of the needs of the children. Green Meadow teachers, school and county administrators, and community parents were brave and wise enough to undertake a change to the public school tradition through a different educational model that served their diverse student population with enormous benefits for teachers.

Teachers learned about year-round or modified-calendar schooling, took ownership over the process, and committed to its success.

Although there were bumps and challenges along the road, that did not deter the teachers in their drive to establish a better learning environment for their students. At this school, the modified calendar motivated teachers to teach and work with a student population that had many needs.

It was refreshing to spend time in a high-needs school where exciting things were happening for children and teachers. The inviting and rigorous academic environment was visible throughout the school and evident in teachers' actions and attitudes.

Year-round or modified-calendar education offered this school a positive and exciting change to better serve children and motivate teachers. This most likely would not have happened without the teachers' commitment to the students, the leadership style of the school administrators, the support from county administrators, and the support from school board members, as well as the Superintendent of Schools, Dr. Daniel Domenech. The transition process that this school orchestrated was highly successful due to many factors. The modified calendar proved to be positive for all at Green Meadow, including the teachers.

CHAPTER 3

New Garden Elementary School

New Garden (pseudonym) was the eighth, and of 2004, the last, school in the county that transitioned from a traditional to a year-round or modified school calendar. This chapter is focused on teachers' motivation and the principal's leadership style during and after that school's transition to a modified calendar.

ABOUT THE SCHOOL

There were approximately 650 students from thirty-six countries who spoke thirty-four different languages enrolled at New Garden. About 280 students qualified for and received services in the school-based ESOL program. The school's staff was comprised of seventy-five teachers, specialists, and instructional assistants. The school qualified for the county's EXCEL program (see chapter 1 for further explanation), but received only partial funding, which was put toward operating the year-round or modified calendar.

On its website, the school is described as "a special needs school, [which] provides an instructional program that meets the educational needs of children and develops lifelong learners." The school's mission statement says that diversity is a "savored strength and [the school] capitalizes on that diversity to challenge all learners. Problem solving is integrated throughout the curriculum as students use problem-based learning to design museums, create math happenings, and explore technology."

One of the unique programs that the school operates is "The New Garden Family Center," which offers family literacy experiences during the school day and evening and day adult literacy education. The school faculty and staff actively involve students and parents beyond the school day through child–parent programs, PTA events, grade-level parent meetings that focus on relevant and practical topics, and an after-school learning assistance program.

During the interviews (see a list of questions in appendix B), the teachers, school administrators, and specialists talked at great length about the reasons the school switched to a modified calendar and the impact that this new calendar had on students and on them. Overall, teachers felt professional enhancement in the quality of their job, which motivated them to want to teach in this high-needs school. A large part of the principal's and assistant principal's discussions included their roles in the transition.

LESSONS LEARNED AT NEW GARDEN ELEMENTARY SCHOOL

The following were themes that emerged from the discussions and observations:

1. The principal's leadership style moved the school to switch to an alternative calendar.
2. Teachers felt less stressed and more motivated under the year-round or modified calendar, mostly because of intersessions.
3. The school administrators and teachers faced challenges in communicating and increasing standardized test scores.

FIRST THEME: THE PRINCIPAL'S LEADERSHIP

In 2001, one of the primary reasons this school switched to a modified calendar was that the principal felt that the students needed more time in school for academic learning, especially since the school's state standardized scores, particularly reading, did not meet the approved benchmark. The initial idea to investigate a change to a modified-calendar format came to the principal from the school's "cluster director" or area supervisor. The cluster director relayed information to the principal about the academic success that other year-round or modified-calendar schools with similar student populations had experienced in the county.

The principal commented, "I'm constantly looking for models to help raise test scores, and I heard about all the success that students had with the model school [Green Meadow School—the county's first year-round education school. See chapter 2.]."

The principal also implied that there was a strong suggestion by county administrators that schools with lagging standardized test scores and a student population similar to that at Green Meadow should look at the year-round or modified-calendar model.

After the principal decided to look at the modified-calendar format, she called on a few teachers and asked them to visit the county pilot school (Green Meadow) and gather information on their transition process and what it entailed. The principal did this by sharing her idea with a few teachers. She added: "I told my teachers, you know, let's get a study group around this idea and whoever is interested should join. We had about fifteen to eighteen teachers who came forward."

One teacher described their task: "The principal put a little bug in a few of our ears and she formed a small committee of about fifteen people to serve on it. She asked us to research the idea over the summer and come back to her with conclusions."

The principal also provided reading materials to the teachers on the committee, and she requested that everyone read them before the next meeting.

The group of teachers liked the program at Green Meadow and felt the principal was on the right track. Then, the principal began convincing the entire New Garden faculty and staff to move to the modified-calendar schedule. The principal invited Green Meadow teachers and the intersession coordinator to a New Garden faculty assembly, so that New Garden teachers could ask questions and discuss the benefits that the calendar held for children and staff.

After several more months of in-house discussions, the next step was the official faculty vote or survey. The ballot was worded in an interesting manner, and the principal explained it this way:

I told my staff we can't go to the community before we, ourselves, decide that this is what's best for the children. We used the voting survey that other schools used and we changed it a little. Teachers had "yes or no questions" on whether this fits their lifestyles and whether it's best for children. So I had about 82–85 percent in favor or "yes" and I had one who said [no] something about lifestyle and six who [said no] thought it's too soon.

Ultimately, only about five teachers eventually left the school after it changed to a modified calendar. After the faculty vote, the principal knew she was going to need to advocate forcefully to the school board for final approval for the transition because the county had put a temporary budget freeze on any new school initiatives, which included year-round or modified-calendar schools.

After the school faculty voted, the next year involved the principal garnering supportive Parent-Teacher Association (PTA) members to back the decision for the school calendar switch. Also, the school held community/parent meetings and worked on the logistics of the process.

In the first community/parent meeting, the principal invited parents from Green Meadow to talk about the modified calendar to the New Garden parents, but unfortunately, only six people showed up for the presentation. However, for the second community/parent meeting, the principal used creativity to ensure a successful community/parent vote because parents had to approve the plan in order for the process to continue through the county's procedures.

One evening, the whole school community was invited to see a magician perform for the children while the principal addressed the parents. The magician idea worked very well because 200 people showed up for the event. The principal's remarks were translated in four other languages and close to 90 percent of the parents voted for the school to change to a modified calendar.

After upper-level county administrators approved New Garden's transition to a modified calendar, teachers felt that they had to continue to fight and persuade the school board in order to be certain the approval was followed out, especially in light of the budget cuts. Lastly, the principal had to lobby school board members to be certain that the funding was available.

The principal knew this would be challenging, and she employed several techniques to win over the board. For example, she talked privately with several school board members. She also furnished to parents the addresses and e-mail addresses of board members and hinted that the parents needed to contact board members. Also she met with the Superintendent of Schools, Dr. Daniel Domenech, on at least one occasion. While involved in that process she was also having conversations with teachers to assure that they were on board with her and the plan.

After a year of crusading, the principal was given the approval by the school board to change calendars. Extra funding was granted to the school through the county EXCEL program (see chapter 1); however, due to the budgetary difficulties that year, New Garden was given only about half of EXCEL money they had expected to receive.

The assistant principal explained it this way:

> In order to be a modified-calendar school [in the county], you have to be an EXCEL school. We were supposed to be EXCEL, but what happened is, when the school board voted, there was not enough money to make us a full EXCEL school. So, they voted to give the modified-calendar funding [to pay for the coordinator and intersession teachers] and they also voted to give us the Waterford reading literacy program for kindergarten and first grades. That's it. We didn't get all the other stuff that we were supposed to.

Finally, the transition was undertaken after two years of preparatory efforts. However, the school was ready at the end of the first year, but the board and county administrators requested that the school faculty and principal take a second year, as had Green Meadow, to prepare more. That additional year proved to be extremely valuable for the staff and administration in preparing the school and community for the new modified-calendar schedule.

The county helped the school transition in many ways. The New Garden intersession coordinator stated,

> They [county administrators] helped us with the food services and transportation, but there were and are still many issues to resolve such as, the "gifted and talented" training for teachers and IEP deadlines which very often follow the traditional calendar and fall during intersessions.

In retrospect, it was abundantly clear to the teachers that the principal championed the whole process and without her drive and determination the change most likely would not have happened. As one teacher put it, ". . . she [the principal] was the catalyst behind it all."

Teachers expressed great admiration for the principal, particularly with regard to her dedication to the school. The principal was well liked and many teachers noted her style fit with the student population. One example was her visibility around the school; she was often seen greeting children and helping teachers in their classes. Teachers felt that she was always approachable and responsive to their needs, which was part of her commitment to move to a modified-calendar school model.

Principal's Leadership Style

This principal had held that position at New Garden since 1989, which was considered a long tenure in the county for a principal at one school. This principal's leadership style was a combination of transformation leadership (Bass, 1985) with a motivational strategy that was clearly goal setting (Locke and Latham, 1990). Goal setting has been found to have positive effects on group and individual motivation. Goal setting is structured in a top-down approach, which attempts to motivate and integrate the efforts of participants toward common goals that are set at higher administration levels. The New Garden principal had the professional capacity, communication skills, and rapport to create an effective leadership style using goal setting.

The teachers held the principal's reputation in high regard. One teacher commented, "She [the principal] has devoted her life to this school. She gives every ounce of herself to make this school better for students and teachers."

As for transformational leading, the principal defined the need for the school calendar to change, created the vision, rallied teachers and parents to commit to the vision, and concentrated on the big picture or long-range goals while attending to the smaller details. As for the teachers, they commended her for taking charge of the process and leading the way. Even the faculty ballots were worded in such a way as to clearly show that the principal was moving in this direction.

One teacher noted that the faculty survey or ballot asked: "Do you think it [the modified calendar] is a good model for children? If yes, are you going to stay?" It was apparent to the teachers that the principal was going ahead with the alternative-calendar plan regardless of the results of the survey. The principal carefully worded the ballot so there was still a consensus or yes or no vote. She followed the county's established procedures faithfully and made clear to teachers that if someone was not on board with her plan, then they had the choice to transfer to another school with a traditional calendar.

Another teacher said that the principal presented the plan to the faculty and said, "If the calendar doesn't fit your personal life because of your children being on the traditional calendar or because you're working on an advanced degree [via a university cohort summer program], then you need to find a different school."

Despite the principal's direct approach, teachers admired her leadership style and felt she supported them as teachers. They also had no resentment or hard feelings about the firm tactics she employed during the whole process. On the contrary, those who remained sought the benefits of the modified calendar, especially the additional days of learning for their students through intersession classes.

Her long-standing presence in the county also helped win the approval of the school board, despite the fact that the school budget was tightened and many new programs in the county were not being funded. The teachers respected her advocacy for their cause. This principal's approach to leadership and motivation was a good example of the importance of interpersonal relationships between leaders and followers. Without such negotiating and communication skills an authoritarian structure may have developed and eclipsed her plan to move the school to a year-round or modified-calendar format with the teachers' full support.

One of the principal's prime objectives was to raise students' standardized test scores by switching to a year-round or modified calendar. She also wanted the teachers to understand and believe in this plan and be involved in the process. Teachers actually felt comforted by the principal's actions and thought that her actions fully supported their efforts as classroom teachers.

One teacher said:

> You can go to the principal with any request as long as you explain your needs and are vocal about it. I feel like when they [principal and assistant principal] can, they do, and they do a great job, but I think also we [teachers] just have to ask and keep asking and then you'll get what you need. We've gotten planning days because we've demonstrated a need for planning days.

SECOND THEME: TEACHER MOTIVATION

In 2004, New Garden was in its second year on the modified calendar, and the teachers started to see the academic impact that the transition had on the children. Also, by the end of the second year, the school became fully accredited by the Virginia Department of Education and won the Governor's Award for "The Most Improved School." The award was based on several factors, including a raise in state standardized test scores. Teachers and administrators took pride in the improved learning outcome at the school. Many teachers explained the change was a result of their hard work as teachers and the twenty-four to thirty extra days of instruction that children received during intersession classes.

Intersessions

It was clear that teachers felt that the most outstanding professional benefit for them was the intersessions, particularly the academic support for the students and the professional options that the intersessions spawned for teachers. At this school, teachers felt a heavy burden on them to increase students' standardized test scores, particularly in light of the No Child Left Behind (NCLB) policy and the state standards. *The academic goal of switching to an alternative calendar was to give students up to thirty more days in school in order to raise standardized test scores.* The intersessions made teachers feel that they were not left on their own to devise a plan to raise scores and that there was actually help and assistance for students.

The intersession coordinator was skilled and well organized, and the intersession classes at New Garden were thoughtfully aligned with the state SOLs. Along with other course offerings, there were many remedial classes for the students such as reteaching and reviewing major concepts and topics. It was interesting to note that the intersession classes at this school heavily revolved around remediation.

One teacher noted, "The real thinking was there was so much information out there that said those [intersession classes] might be a good way to help our students achieve. It [intersession classes] is by providing more time in school. We had that evidence from the pilot school [Green Meadow]."

Many young teachers wanted to work as intersession instructors since there was an opportunity to earn money in addition to their annual salary. Teachers earned approximately $1,000 extra for each two-week intersession class they taught.

Another benefit of the intersession classes for new teachers was that they had the opportunity to try a variety of alternative teaching methods. With accountability in mind, many of the newer teachers tended to hesitate during the regular school instructional time when using different methods of teaching.

Also, newer teachers expressed excitement over selecting favorite subjects or topics to present in a hands-on or constructivist approach. The professional challenge of constructivist teaching was appealing, and the extra income was the icing on the cake. Many of the newer teachers thought that intersession classes seemed to be a better opportunity for them to earn extra money and implement an alternative teaching strategy rather than having to commit to teaching a whole summer school session on the traditional calendar.

A mentor teacher for new teachers described that process:

There was a teacher who taught a science class during one intersession. Honestly, it was the way science ought to be taught . . . every day of the week. . . . [It worked out during the intersession class] because of the increased opportunity for freedom, for choice on curriculum, for choice in teaching methods.

The teacher highlighted in the above example felt that she was able to teach in that manner because of the environment provided during intersessions. All intersession classes were clearly aligned with standards, and teachers were encouraged to use hands-on experiences and cut out the more traditional "textbook" instruction. Many teachers chose to work intersessions because it was different than their regular teaching and because they could teach a different grade level, teach mornings or afternoons, and there was less pressure involved. This actually helped the teachers return to school refreshed and renewed, even though they had just worked another two weeks!

The assistant principal talked about the careful planning that goes into all the intersession classes. "There aren't any 'fluff' classes. There just can't be. If you're teaching a cheerleading class or a race car class, it *still* has to focus on reading, writing, and math, and you have to think about how you're going to get those objectives in [the curriculum]."

He went on to explain the crucial role of the intersession coordinator: "So, that's where Nancy (pseudonym) [intersession coordinator] comes in, trying to help those teachers to create a class syllabus and plan some lessons that are focused on the essential knowledge and skills. It's hard, but I think we're getting much better at it."

As for faculty teaching during intersessions, the intersession coordinator was careful not to exert pressure on teachers, including new teachers. However, the coordinator did give preference to the in-house teachers if they desired to instruct an intersession class. There was also a pool of retired professionals or teachers on family leave or maternity leave from the county who thoroughly enjoyed teaching for two weeks every three months.

A New Garden specialist, who was also a new teacher mentor, expressed this sentiment: "With four weeks to go in the first quarter they [new teachers] see the end. They see a break in October, which follows nine weeks of instruction. That's a huge benefit because in a regular year calendar school all they can look for in October is Thanksgiving break."

As for teachers who did not work as intersession instructors, the breaks away from school worked to their advantage in several ways. The two-week respites spread out over the year provided blocks of nine weeks of teaching time, which was manageable, especially for new teachers. Teachers felt less continuous pressure because of the frequent breaks.

Regardless as to whether the teachers were rookies or veterans, many chose not to teach during intersessions. Instead those teachers used the time to relax, rejuvenate, travel, and enjoy seasonal sightseeing excursions. One teacher, new to the area, used the intersession breaks to tour Washington and go to museums, the mountains, and beaches. Another teacher took the October intersession as an opportunity to enjoy autumn by taking day trips to the mountains, something he had never done during his many years as a teacher in a traditional-calendar school. These were important benefits for teachers of the high-needs students, who often worked long and sometimes stressful schedules. Many teachers commented that they felt refreshed after the breaks, which positively impacted their teaching and attitudes.

There were two unforeseen disadvantages of the alternative calendar cited by New Garden teachers. The first disadvantage, albeit limited to the first year, was that the faculty had no real summer break the year the school transitioned to the year-round or modified calendar. The traditional school year ended late in June, and then teachers were due back the middle of July to prepare for the August 1 opening.

The second disadvantage expressed by teachers regarded the use of their classrooms by other instructors during intersessions classes. The teachers were frustrated to find that the classrooms were not returned to them in neat and clean shape. However, the intersession coordinator later worked with the outside intersession instructors to rectify the problem and continued to be sure it did not occur again.

THIRD THEME: CHALLENGES—COMMUNICATION AND TEST SCORES

During the years leading up to the school transition, one challenge faced by teachers and administrators was in communicating with parents, and particularly those of newly enrolled students, regarding the change in the schedule. Even after the school operated on this calendar for two years, some parents were still sending their children to school in September instead of August.

Teachers explained the communication troubles as due in part to the high turnover in immigrant and non–English speaking families. The neighborhoods around New Garden tended to have transient families who had limited English language abilities. Many parents who were new to the neighborhood were not aware of the modified-calendar schedule and did not understand it even when it was explained to them.

The communication difficulties also impacted the intersession classes. Again, some parents were not aware of or did not understand that they needed to register their child or children for intersession classes or they would not be able to participate. The school simply could not have children "walk in" to intersession classes because there was a certain teacher–student ratio they had to abide by.

The intersession coordinator described the consequences for some parents who did not register their children in time for the intersession classes. As a result, some of those parents had to find alternative child-care arrangements at the last minute.

Consequently, the faculty continued to work on parental outreach and education programs that would lead to better communication between the school and family. The teachers and principal found that it was not simply just a matter of furnishing translated materials to the parents. Instead, the teachers learned to capitalize on any contact they had with parents, such as progress conferences or during activities at the school, to reinforce the concepts of the alternative calendar including the format of intersession classes.

Communication challenges were not just with parents. New Garden teachers also cited communication difficulties that arose among themselves, especially for first-year teachers. One teacher said: "I would like to see more collaboration within the school, not just with teams individually but with other grade levels and with the specialists . . . to use and to tap into all those resources. I don't know anyone outside of my group because I never see them."

The physical layout of the school facility was not readily conducive to much regular face-to-face contact, since there were several permanent trailers that housed some grade levels. Also, the main school building was divided into pod areas between two floors. The physical isolation of some teachers from their colleagues limited the occasion and situations when fellow teachers could discuss items of mutual importance concerning students and curriculum. Nevertheless, several teachers responded to this shortcoming by fostering better informal communication and started an after-school knitting club for teachers.

Standardized Test Scores

Teachers expressed that they were under tremendous pressure to increase students' standardized test scores, especially before the school transitioned to the alternative calendar. A major reason that the principal aggressively pursued the switch to a year-round or modified calendar was to give students more time in school (up to thirty additional days), which in turn would help teachers' efforts in the classroom and thus increase the student achievement reflected by the test scores. Early on, teachers recognized the principal's motives for switching school calendars and felt this was indeed a way to meet the students' needs and to increase student achievement.

As one teacher mentioned, "Not a day goes by that I can't help but to think of the [standardized] test scores. . . . Others [schools] in the county know the rankings."

The assistant principal summed up his feelings in this way:

I guess the bottom line in terms of success [with the modified calendar] is standardized tests [scores]. The bottom line is: are your kids achieving and are they doing better? If 85–90 percent of your kids get five extra weeks of instruction and you're lowering the retention issues of a long summer, that should make a difference in their achievement. And so, ultimately, that's what every school is going to be judged on, whatever programs that they implement. Is the average yearly progress for all the different age targets for No Child Left Behind being met? . . . and [is] the requirement for the state of Virginia being met?

REFLECTIONS

Overall, New Garden radiated with energy and friendliness. The office was generally bustling with activity: the staff spoke English and Spanish, and teachers were freely streaming into the office area to talk to the office staff, principal, and assistant principal at various times of the day. Also, there was a feeling of openness, especially from the principal. She immediately responded to the authors' request to develop a case study of the school. When teachers needed to be asked about participating in interviews for the case study, the principal was most accommodating and asked the intersession coordinator to follow through with the requests. The coordinator did—on the same day! The principal was eager to be a part of research that involved her teachers and the year-round or modified-calendar schedule. This principal was found to be most enthusiastic about learning more on motivating teachers under the modified calendar, and she took great personal pride in being a part of the endeavor.

The interviewed teachers, half of whom were rookie teachers, expressed a balanced view of the calendar. They were able to see the many benefits and some challenges. Veteran teachers who were there during the transition expressed enthusiasm about the change and admiration for the principal because of her ability to tirelessly advocate for New Garden students and teachers. The teachers knew that her passion was switching to the year-round or modified calendar for the sake of the students, and they wholeheartedly supported her efforts. Also, teachers supported the principal so readily because of the pressure they felt to increase students' standardized test scores and the perception created by the principal that the modified calendar was a way to help students academically.

The alternative calendar brought several unexpected benefits to New Garden teachers. The intersessions provided several opportunities, particularly for the overwhelming number of first and second-year teachers. It gave the newer teachers a two-week break every quarter or nine weeks, which allowed them to regroup, reflect, and evaluate their own personal progress toward mastery of teaching. The breaks also gave the rookie teachers valuable curriculum planning time. Many untenured and veteran teachers taught intersession classes and found the experience rewarding in numerous ways. It was an opportunity to earn extra income, teach different students, teach a different grade level using a variety of instructional methods, and teach a different subject or topic.

Other teachers used the intersession breaks to relax, travel, and rejuvenate away from school. Many took advantage of off-season travel in October or explored local sites during the off-peak tourist season in the Washington area.

The principal's transformation leadership and goal-setting motivational style, along with her personality traits, amounted to an effective combination in moving the school to successfully transition to the year-round or modified calendar. Teachers described the principal as a visionary leader and committed principal. She knew the modified schedule would be good for the student population and worked tirelessly and diplomatically to bring the teachers on board with her vision, which was quite surprising since the change was more than less from a top-to-bottom flow. Perhaps the teachers knew the limitations of their own lobbying and advocacy capabilities and trusted the principal implicitly in her actions. They had full faith in the end result.

Teachers discussed the "selling points" of the modified calendar to newly recruited teachers interviewing for positions at New Garden. Several teachers pointed out the fact that the school had a largely poor and needy student population, which made it sometimes difficult to attract and retain new teachers, but the alternative calendar was fast becoming an attraction to bring teachers to the school and for them to stay.

The assistant principal mentioned, ". . . we've had more teacher stability [this year] in terms of turnover than any year previous. I don't know if you can take one year in isolation and attribute it to the modified calendar or not, [but] we just didn't have as many teachers go this year."

The challenges the school faced with parental communication was interesting. Even after two years on the alternative calendar, the school was still grappling with the problem of some parents who did not comprehend the start and end dates of the school year. This raised a question: how many of the parents and members of the community really understood the premise of year-round or modified-calendar schooling? There was really only one night that a substantial parental turnout occurred, and parents were informed *and* voted for the switch on this evening. This was remarkable given that the process of communicating such a magnitude of information generally would have taken months. Another point may be that the community was extremely transient and many were not part of the information session two years back. Perhaps a position may need to be created or the job of facilitating this intersession information to new parents be added to a current school/community liaison if it has not already.

Another interesting finding by the teachers was the lack of collaboration among teachers, particularly since other schools on the alternative calendar actually have stated that this model *promotes* teacher collaboration by coteaching and team teaching of intersession classes. However, the opportunity for teachers to engage in team teaching at this school was quite limited. Perhaps as more teachers engage in instructing intersession classes, there may be more team or coteaching opportunities, which may carry over into the regular instructional curriculum.

Standardized testing was the primary catalyst behind New Garden switching to an alternative-calendar school. Within two years on the year-round or modified calendar, the school increased students' standardized test scores to the point that the school became fully accredited in 2004 by the state. In many ways, the school achieved its overarching goal of increasing student achievement, and at the same time learned that the modified calendar had many positive implications for teachers as well.

CHAPTER 4

Westlake Elementary School

SCHOOL DESCRIPTION AND POPULATION

Westlake Elementary School (pseudonym) is located only seven miles from Washington, D.C., and has a diverse population with approximately 900 students from fifty-eight different countries and twenty-three different languages spoken. It was one of the largest elementary schools according to the number of students in the county. There were 414 students in the ESL program, and in 2004, over 40 percent of the students received free and/or reduced-price breakfasts and lunches, which qualified Westlake for Title I funds. There were approximately eighty teachers and specialists, as well as three school administrators.

Westlake was nestled in a neighborhood of single-family homes that were built during the 1960s. At one time the school primarily served that community, but during the 1980s and 1990s, a large commercial corridor, including several high-rise apartment dwellings, was developed adjacent to the school and neighborhood. In 2004, few students from the older neighborhood attended Westlake. Most of the students lived in the apartments and were new to the United States. The original school structure was not designed to educate 900 students, which was the reason that there were several permanent trailer units in the back of the school.

When the work for this case study started, the principal was our first contact with the school. She was exceptionally welcoming and extremely receptive to the idea of her school participating in such a study. She requested that the faculty be apprised of this work at the next full faculty meeting. After a brief presentation at the meeting, interested teachers were asked to write their names and e-mail addresses so they could be contacted later for a voluntary interview.

Including the formal tape-recorded interview, there were also several informal discussions with the principal. She talked candidly and went into detail about Westlake as an EXCEL school (see chapter 1) and its plan to include a school-wide focus on literacy—a mandated, uninterrupted ninety-minute period for reading and writing every day with "Reading Recovery" trained teachers and specialists embedded in every classroom. She identified the challenges facing her, the faculty, and students. She was quite impressive in regards to her personal warmth and intelligence, and the fact she took over as principal during the fourth month of the first year the school began on a modified calendar!

LESSONS LEARNED AT WESTLAKE

The following were the three main themes:

1. Teacher motivation focused on the modified calendar and ways it inspired, and/or simply made teaching a better professional and personal experience at Westlake.
2. There were several obstacles or setbacks that Westlake administration and faculty faced during the pre- and post-transition from a traditional school to a modified-calendar school.
3. The second principal came on board several months into the new calendar and was more effective with the task at hand.

FIRST THEME: TEACHER MOTIVATION

Teachers were excited and sparked to be teaching at this modified-calendar school, mostly because of the intersessions, the classes, and the breaks spread out throughout the year. The benefits that they discussed in detail were the opportunity to earn extra money teaching an intersession class or classes, teaming and coteaching classes during intersession, chances for off-season travel, "uncluttered" professional reflection and destressing time, the educational benefit for students, intersession classes that supported their classroom instruction, and online M.Ed. courses.

Along with the regular vacations (Thanksgiving recess, winter break, and spring break) scheduled by the county, the modified calendar afforded four weeks off in the summer (instead of ten weeks), two weeks in October, two weeks in January, and two weeks in March or April depending on the county spring break.

The breaks throughout the twelve months were of tremendous assistance in relieving the daily, chronic stress and burnout many Westlake teachers said they faced when they worked with a high-needs population. The breaks gave teachers time to relax and restore energy, and it also helped to reaffirm the value of their commitment to teach students who had limited English and other challenges brought to school from their home environments. One teacher commented, "After two weeks I was ready to see my students; I missed them."

With the breaks at unusual times, such as October and March or April, teachers liked the opportunities to take personal time when their own children were at school and/or their spouses were not home. One teacher shared how she worked outside in her garden for most of the break during the spring. She said, "I love this time for just me. I planted my flower garden and just puttered around outside without a lot of distractions from my family. I'm looking forward to it again this year."

Off-season travel was another bonus that teachers liked about the modified calendar. One teacher visited China in October and found the trip exhilarating and reasonably priced. She explained that she never had opportunities to travel with her husband during the fall when tourists tend to be fewer and prices for overseas trips fall considerably. With many of their own children grown, several veteran teachers enjoyed the option of travel during the intersession or breaks and felt this was a definite advantage for teaching at a modified-calendar school.

Several other veteran teachers felt the breaks throughout the year gave them time to focus on elderly parents residing out of town. A teacher commented, "I like to visit my folks in Florida and focus on them . . . when it's not a holiday or summer." Another teacher talked about herself and her sister caring for their parents several hours away. She said, "The breaks give me time to check on their medication, schedule doctor's visits with them, and look into home repairs. We figured out that someone can be with them for about a week nearly every month—she takes September, me October, she November, both of us in December, me in January, she in February, me in March or

April, she in May. . . . It's more doable than when I had all this time in the summer and I was squeezing visits in over long weekends. I was stressed and resentful and something had to give."

Two younger teachers (they had less than five years of teaching experience) used the breaks throughout the year to work on professional goals such as an online M.Ed. degree. One teacher said, "I'm taking two graduate courses online a semester, and I do most of my graduate work during the breaks." She commented that this time was better suited for her since it was away from holidays, which helped her to focus on the goal of a master's degree.

Another way the modified calendar motivated teachers was through the enrichment and remediation classes offered to students during intersessions. Around 70 percent of Westlake students enrolled in intersession classes, and teachers felt that this was the best emotional, social, and academic investment for their students. One teacher commented, ". . . regardless of the class, students are exposed to English—written and spoken—and this is a plus no matter what class they take during intersession."

The teachers also realized that the modified calendar allowed students to better retain the information from their regular classes, and this helped them to be more positive in their teaching efforts. They explained that the "flow" of the curriculum was smoother, which meant fewer review or reteaching lessons, especially in September. Before Westlake went to a modified calendar, teachers said that in the fall they would often review for four or six weeks and work intensively on language skills since many of the students had had little exposure to English over the nine weeks of summer vacation.

The intersession classes also gave struggling students remediation opportunities with another teacher who could present the curriculum in a different way or style. Teachers commented that this usually helped students see that another teacher cared about their education and tried to teach them the same material they had learned in the classroom but in perhaps a different way. This helped students to see that the whole school was a positive place where multiple adults cared about them and their learning.

Many of the intersession classes implemented a hands-on approach that tapped into students' multiple senses. Howard Gardner's multiple intelligences theory (1983) was seen as a guide for methodology in several of the remediation intersession classes. One teacher, who taught a remediation class, commented that those classes were lighter in terms of stress and more fun for students. It was not an "intense time," and students responded academically to this atmosphere better, she thought.

Many teachers commented that the intersessions helped relieve their day-to-day stress that often built over time in situations where large numbers of students were making progress but still functioning at below grade level, especially in reading and writing. Whether the teachers taught an intersession class or not, many shared the importance of intersession classes as a support to their own classroom efforts.

Most of the teachers who chose to work at least one intersession class throughout the year had less than five years of experience. Most of those teachers commented that the opportunities were predominately driven by the incentive to earn extra income. Also, those same teachers enjoyed coteaching with other more experienced teachers from a different grade level. This gave them an opportunity to learn "on the job" from another teacher without committing to a longer, more elaborate coteaching arrangement. What happened, though, is that several pairs clicked, and their relationship continued after the intersession and coteaching commitment ended. As one teacher explained, "Without so many curriculum pressures during intersessions, we could be a little more creative and explorative with our coteaching partner . . . we could try some different methods or styles that maybe we wouldn't do in the classroom during the year."

Teachers who worked intersessions often felt invigorated and looked forward to returning to their regular classrooms after the break. One teacher said, "I had a great time in my intersession class. I did something called "literary chefs." We read a story and then we cooked! For example, we read *The Very Hungry Caterpillar* and then made 'caterpillar' no-bake cookies. Literacy, language, math, all kinds of skills were united and built on each other during the lesson." Other teachers commented that working with other students in a different grade level made the intersession classes interesting. For example, a couple of teachers in the primary grades thought working with students in the upper grades would be interesting and give them a different perspective in regards to the curriculum, student learning, and second language development.

Other coteaching opportunities during intersession included teachers on maternity leave who wanted to stay connected with teaching but also wanted to take off time for their family. The coteaching model helped them to feel connected with a practicing teacher and utilize their time more efficiently. Also, the intersession classes were divided into morning and afternoon classes, which gave the teachers more flexibility if they chose only to teach a morning or an afternoon or both.

To summarize, the modified calendar and intersessions gave teachers many opportunities to feel invigorated and motivated in their teaching. Most teachers found that the breaks distributed throughout the year provided a time to travel, focus on family, destress and reflect, teach other grades and topics in an intersession class, coteach or team teach an intersession class, complete online master's degree course work, earn extra money through teaching an intersession class, and supported their endeavors teaching high-needs students. Teachers felt that the remediation and enrichment intersession classes were one of the most important aspects of the modified-calendar format since students had opportunities to continue and reinforce classroom learning on a more even schedule.

SECOND THEME: A FEW OBSTACLES— THE TRANSITION AND TEST SCORES

Although the intersessions were a significant motivating factor with teachers at Westlake, there were also several rough patches that West-lake teachers experienced. The first was the transition process from a traditional to a modified-calendar school under the former principal.

In 2000, after two years on an extended school day schedule, the former principal and a handful of teachers felt that that strategy was not meeting the challenge of ESOL students, particularly those students who would leave Westlake midwinter to go to the family's native country for two or three months and then return at the end of the school year, usually right before the county and state testing time. Both teachers and the former principal felt that the students' extended absence often undermined the teachers' efforts.

According to the former principal, she would attend monthly meetings with the principals from the other EXCEL program (see chapter 1) schools to see what they were doing to extend learning time. She kept hearing positive comments about the modified-calendar schools (particularly the intersessions) that were also EXCEL schools, in meeting the academic needs of the schools' large ESOL populations.

According to the former principal, after a year of discussion and study, the majority of faculty voted to implement the modified calendar; however, nearly all of the teachers saw the year of discussion and study differently. It was never clear to the teachers as to the specific reasons for exploring and ultimately switching to a modified-calendar school since the school's standardized test scores were already increasing under the original EXCEL plan. Several of the teachers who worked at Westlake before and during all the changes in curriculum and instruction under the county's EXCEL mandate felt that the modified-calendar idea definitely had roots with the principal and not with the faculty.

It is a fact, that there were some discussion meetings with teachers and parents, and eventually, there was a faculty vote. Many teachers were dismayed at the whole process, including the faculty vote. One teacher explained, "Our [former] principal really wanted year-round school. . . . I'm like, 'Why are so many people [teachers] leaving if everyone voted for this?'"

Westlake teachers expressed surprise that the modified-calendar faculty vote passed by a majority since an informal poll amongst them revealed the opposite result. When teachers pressed for a recount or a faculty member as an overseer, Westlake's administration reacted with ambiguity. Many teachers felt unsatisfied with the vote and outcome. Nevertheless, the outcome stood and Westlake moved into a modified calendar in 2002.

In 2002, twenty-seven out of eighty Westlake teachers and specialists left Westlake and opted for the county's assistance in transfers to other schools in the county with a traditional calendar. The reasons were not exactly clear why a large number of faculty members left or transferred from Westlake, but several teachers revealed that there was a general dissatisfaction with the former principal's administration style, particularly her push for the modified calendar. One teacher mentioned, "A number of people left because there was some unhappiness with the [former] principal . . . there was a fair amount of dissatisfaction." For public consumption, most teachers cited, "to be closer to home" as their reason for leaving.

As one person stated, "When a whole department leaves, then typically it's administration. For a whole ESOL department to leave at once—it's huge—and the third-grade team left as well. That means there were some conflicting philosophies."

Significantly, the principal who had led the campaign to transition Westlake to a modified-calendar school transferred to another school after only several months into the first year on the modified calendar. Also, the assistant principal went to another county school after the first year. The departures struck many teachers as incompatible with the need for stable leadership to guide faculty members and the school with continuity though the crucial transition period. However, the former principal explained that the county asked her to become principal at another school where her skills were needed and she was ready for the new challenge.

The faculty who stayed on for the transition commented on the difficulty of coming back so quickly to teach school during the first summer. The regular calendar ended in late June, and then by August 1, the school and teachers had to be ready to begin the school year as a modified-calendar school. Several teachers felt this was the most stressful time in many ways and were glad when the October intersession gave a two-week break.

The increased focus on standardized testing and the students' scores led to increased stress, according to teachers. There were many changes and transfers with administration, faculty, curriculum, and students that occurred at Westlake during the first year of the modified-calendar school year. Taken altogether, teachers felt that the changes negatively impacted faculty morale, trust, motivation, and school climate.

Changes also occurred within the school's student population, and this seemed to affect the standardized test scores that were closely monitored by the county and state. The current principal explained that "last year [the first year of the modified calendar] . . . our opt-out students [who transferred] to Iron Run (pseudonym) are students who have parents who work with them, who are from more middle-class families . . . that alone could affect a lot of the [test] scores." She went on and said, "Three of the kids that one of the mothers moved out [to Iron Run] last year, [those] children had all achieved 'pass-advance' on the SOLs [standards of learning], and a great deal more points are given [from the county's ranking] to a school achievement index on the 'pass-advance.'"

By 2003, teachers were able to look back and reflect over the years from 2000 to 2002. They felt that the change in the principal and assistant principal was a positive one, and that the modified calendar was definitely the right model for them and their students. The teachers who stayed on the faculty past the transition to a modified-calendar school expressed positive sentiments for the new school administration. However, those teachers were also realistic and pragmatic. They knew that the state standardized test scores would have a significant impact on whether Westlake remained a modified-calendar school in the future.

THIRD THEME: THE SCHOOL LEADERSHIP

Westlake had a unique situation: essentially two principals impacted the school's transition before and after it became a modified-calendar school.

The first principal's style was mostly characteristic of an authoritarian structure because of the impersonal directives and decisions made by her with little or no impact from the teachers. Before and during the transition period, professional motivation and faculty morale were low because many teachers felt that their ideas and concerns were not seriously considered by the principal. With little or no faith in the principal, many teachers opted for what they saw as their only real choice: transfer to another school within the county.

When the second principal took office in November, she had an extremely difficult task at hand. Not only did she need to lead the school through the remainder of the first year as a modified-calendar school, but she also needed to regain the teachers' trust, buoy faculty morale, and focus on curriculum issues relating to the school's standardized test scores. Definitely not an easy job for someone! She needed to work quickly on major issues and gain the trust of the faculty.

The second principal's leadership style was best described as transactional. This was probably the most effective style to implement for the situation at hand. She needed teachers to rapidly buy into the modified calendar since it was already in place, and faculty was then not wholeheartedly in agreement with it. She needed to motivate the teachers by exchanging "rewards" for their "teaching" or services. She spent a great amount of time with teachers in teams, individually, and as a whole faculty to determine what are their needs. Once she determined what they needed, for example, instructional support or curriculum support, she went to work. The principal met with grade-level teams and worked with the trainers to ensure that the Literacy Collaborative Program from Ohio State University was being implemented in a systematic and effective manner. She supported the teachers' needs in exchange for those teachers' support of the modified calendar and increasing standardized tests scores.

Westlake had over eighty teachers and was one of the largest elementary schools in the county. The sheer size of the faculty compounded the second principal's challenges. However, by the second year of operation as a modified-calendar school, the principal had started to turn the school around instructionally, and the results were reflected in the teachers and the students. One teacher said, "I was ready to bail out of here after the first year [of the modified calendar] because of all the instability. But I didn't because I really like Natalie (pseudonym) [the second principal]. She speaks fluent Spanish, cares about our kids, the community, and us—the teachers!"

REFLECTIONS

Not unlike many other schools in the county, Westlake experienced some difficulties in coming to terms with the changing demographics of its student population. Until the modified-calendar format was presented, it seemed that the school never came to a united decision on the overarching mission and direction for educating lower-income students with limited or no English proficiency. Even though the modified-calendar format was adopted in a less than ideal manner, the faculty members who stayed at Westlake were ultimately positive about it and recognized the many benefits it had for them.

After two years on the modified-calendar format, a sense of promise and optimism was found amongst the teachers. They were beginning to recognize through their own firsthand experiences that the modified calendar was a good fit for them and their students. Also, a sense of pride became evident throughout the school. The teachers and students knew that they were implementing something different, trying something different, and in some ways charting new waters, all under the gifted and strong leadership of the second principal.

The modified calendar was the vehicle or framework that was used to make many other changes throughout the school, including curriculum changes and the addition of new faculty members who brought "fresh eyes" to the school. The faculty who stayed after the school calendar was modified were pleasantly surprised that the modified calendar brought so many rewarding aspects to their jobs, such as a renewed purpose or energy in their daily lessons.

The teachers found that the most important bonus for them under this format was time—time for themselves, time to plan appropriate lessons, time to meet the needs of their students, time to read professional journals and engage in professional dialogue, time to take a critical look at themselves and the curriculum, and time to enjoy being with children and teaching.

The new principal spent many hours with faculty on the newly adopted school-wide literacy curriculum, and she knew it was hard for teachers to change. She stated, "Many teachers in our primary grades are used to 'hobby teaching.' This is when they teach all about apples in the fall and show certain videos and read books on apples. This might be okay at another school, but here [at Westlake] we need to focus on the students and their needs. I don't allow videos in the primary grades at all because students stop talking, stop being engaged, and our students need to be engaged in language arts and literacy every possible moment that they are here [at school]."

The commitment and dedication to the school, students, and faculty, as shown by the new principal who inherited the challenges, was impressive. She did not seek out the principal's job but was invited by county administrators to apply for the position.

Teachers shared many anecdotal stories of their day-to-day struggles in teaching lower-income students with limited or no English language ability in a field that measures academic success through state standardized tests that are also taken by students at neighboring schools where language challenges may not necessarily be present.

One teacher described the standardized test writing prompt given to students during the prior year. There was a big treasure chest in the middle of the room, and students were asked to write about the chest. Where could it have come from? Who could have possibly owned it? The students were given the word "chest," and many reactively looked it up in the dictionary and went to the first definition, which describes "chest" as part the human body. So, those students thought to write about the treasure chest as part of the human body. As a result, many of the students failed that portion of the test.

The teacher was extremely upset but knew there was nothing she could do. She thought if there was some effort made to at least describe the different meanings of the same word, then maybe the students could have been tested more accurately. The teacher was optimistic that the intense literacy curriculum (Ohio State's Literacy Collaborative Program) focus offered with the intersession classes could amount to a powerful combination that might empower Westlake students to achieve higher levels of English literacy.

The intersessions were the most important component of the modified calendar. The intersessions gave students the extended learning time in the classroom and gave teachers a variety of options that would fit their needs and purposes—professionally and personally. Teachers liked having these choices. It gave them more control over their time and how they wanted to use it. The modified calendar was one way to use time more effectively and creatively, without extending teacher contract days for the year.

Several teachers commented that the modified calendar made their elderly parent caring tasks more manageable and even rewarding by allowing them to assist their parents during times of the year other than traditional holidays and school breaks. Other professions assist their employees with support and release time for the care of elderly parents, but it is harder for traditional-calendar schools to do the same. Also, the modified calendar may be beneficial in districts where there are many teachers approaching retirement age and who may have elderly parental care responsibilities. The personal time flexibility of the modified calendar may be useful in keeping those veteran or master teachers in the profession for several more years.

Today, there are literally dozens of accredited online graduate programs available to teachers in all parts of the country. The modified-calendar format could assist teachers who want to pursue a specialist's or master's degree. The breaks throughout the year are an ideal time to complete coursework. Also, many urban districts need to hire provisionally certified teachers with the agreement that the new hire will earn a teaching or master's degree within a certain number of years. The modified calendar may be a way that districts can support those teachers who enroll in an online degree program.

Much of the curriculum was compactly structured to teach the standards that encompass information found on the state standardized tests. Teachers commented that there was little time to expand on students' interests or teachers' unique skills or knowledge before the modified calendar was implemented. However, intersessions gave teachers the opportunity to share a specific talent or skill, such as knitting or cooking, interwoven with a literacy component in an environment that was less stressful for them and the students. These enrichment and remedial classes augmented the school, county, and state curricula. Interessions lowered everyone's (teachers', students', and even administrators') stress levels and allowed students to feel that school was a place where they wanted to go, not simply a place they were obligated to go. Also, intersessions consisted of interesting, stimulating lessons, which allowed students to go more in-depth into topics through hands-on experiences over a two-week period.

Even though faculty morale was low at Westlake during and right after the transition to a modified-calendar school, there were signs after the first year as a modified-calendar school that morale was on the upswing, mostly because of the changes in the school administration and the positive leadership that the new principal and vice principal demonstrated.

Also, morale was increasing because of team teaching and coteaching opportunities that the modified calendar presented to Westlake teachers. Many teachers were coteaching and teaming together for the first time and realized the benefits for students, faculty, and themselves. There was a sense that the faculty was encouraged to come together in teams not only for the required curriculum but also for intersession courses. Several teachers commented that in the past they rarely teamed because there never seemed to be time to plan and implement lessons as a team throughout the year. The teachers said that the modified-calendar format assisted them in making team teaching more practicable.

There were many teachers at Westlake who had little or no prior teaching experience. Many had just graduated with a teaching license, and this was their first teaching job. Other Title I or high-needs schools, especially in inner-city or urban areas face the same predicament: newly graduated teachers are placed in schools with high-needs or at-risk students who have many academic and personal challenges because more experienced teachers tend to transfer to non–high needs schools. The modified calendar can be a way to bring a better or healthier balance to a school faculty. The modified calendar has benefits for veteran as well as untenured teachers. Students also benefit by the variety of experiences of the teachers as well.

At Westlake, energy and excitement was evident amongst the teachers. They liked teaching. Even though they were practical and realistic, they were enthusiastic about their jobs and teaching high-needs students. Several Westlake teachers had been teaching for many years and commented that the modified calendar gave them precious time to regroup, rest, reflect, and be the best teacher they could be.

Westlake had several bumps and challenges to face before, during, and after the transition to a modified calendar, but they had turned the corner on that chapter. Teachers at Westlake will continue to benefit in numerous ways as a result of the modified calendar, and this will impact their teaching, which will ultimately have a positive effect on their students.

CHAPTER 5

An Action Plan: Getting Started

WHY SCHOOLS SWITCH

Many schools decide to switch to a modified calendar to take advantage of the increased instructional time for students obtainable through intersessions. Additionally, schools may make the transaction in order to lessen summer learning loss and to meet other needs of both students and teachers. Teachers everywhere face a common problem: how to teach massive amounts of curriculum in 180 days to students who have unique language and other learning needs. Those seeking a change find that the modified-calendar format consisting of four forty-five school day sessions from August 1 through June 30 with two-week intersessions as a good remedy.

The intersessions provide for students to spend up to an additional thirty thirty days in the classroom. Those additional days offer more time for student reinforcement and enrichment. Also, the modified calendar has shown to inspire and motivate teachers who work with high-needs students.

Think about what motivates your school to change to a modified calendar. Consider the following questions:

- Why do your students need more time in the classroom for learning?
- Do some of the students regress academically, socially, and emotionally over the breaks and summer vacation under your traditional calendar?
- Are you seeking intrinsic benefits for teachers: stress reduction and increased motivation?
- Is the year-round or modified-calendar schedule a potential match for your teachers, students, and community?

Step One

The first step in transforming a traditional-calendar school to a year-round or modified calendar is to assemble a core group of teachers to spearhead the project. It is important to remember that a grassroots effort is involved at most schools that successfully transition from a traditional model to a year-round or modified-calendar schedule. The effort begins with the teachers and principals and works its way upward through the greater school community to culminate with the approval of the school board. Members of the core group should initially be tasked to investigate the year-round or modified-calendar concept to determine if that concept is appropriate for their school. In other words, they should do some homework.

It is also important to include parents, community members, and county or school district administrators early on in the process. Instead of addressing the entire parental community early on, think about inviting a handful of parents, such as the PTA leadership, into the early discussions, and let those parents assist with the information gathering. If the school–parent outreach is stronger through a community liaison, have the liaison gather a group of parents. Another idea is to form a "think tank" or informal committee of people who are interested in discussing and exploring the idea.

Dividing the core group into subgroups with specific tasks is a good way to maximize time and resources. One group may research modified-calendar schools and student achievement, the second group can look at intersessions and their curriculum, and the third group can develop a plan to engage community and parental support on a grander scale. All three subgroups need to attend conferences, read current literature, and visit with teachers at modified-calendar schools. Be certain to maintain the focus on the reasons for the change.

The resources of The National Association for Year-Round Education (NAYRE) provide an excellent starting point for individuals or schools when looking into a transition to a year-round or modified calendar (there is a resource list following this chapter that lists books, articles, websites, modified-calendar schools, and associations). NAYRE has a publication, *Year-Round Education Resource Guidebook*, which provides some basic guidelines to consider before moving toward a decision. Also, NAYRE holds an annual conference in San Diego, California, which features presentation sessions where educators from around North America meet and exchange ideas and research results on year-round and modified-calendar schools.

The organization's 2004 conference included presentations by superintendents, principals, teachers, and teacher educators who are all involved in year-round or modified-calendar schools. The topics ranged from coordinating intersessions, school success stories, and student achievement. Also, NAYRE organizes regional meetings in various locations throughout the United States.

Schools who have demonstrated the most success in smoothly transitioning to a modified calendar format had teachers who spearheaded the change and allowed about three years for the whole process. Faculty retreats are a good place to begin frank discussions and share literature on modified-calendar schools. Remember, the entire faculty may not initially agree, but it is important to include all faculty voices early on. The change will not occur overnight; it is a long process that must be thought all the way through in order to ensure success.

In short, schools experience problems when there is not consensus among faculty, parents, or the community in the early stages and throughout the process. Also, schools that move too quickly (less than two years) have shown difficultly in transitions or unsuccessful transitions.

Step Two

After a year of researching, discussing, debating, and visiting successful modified-calendar schools, the next step is to bring the plan to the larger community and parents. As one school's administrator put it, "It was the political year." It is important for the faculty to be united at this stage, which likely entails polling the faculty for a majority vote to serve as a mandate to move the plan forward.

At one of the case study schools, a series of five meetings were held at different times—after school, in the evening, and on Saturdays. Prior to the meetings, the principal, assistant principal, and several teachers were trained to learn how to be productive facilitators, so that every parent or community member could express their views—positive or negative. Fliers with times and dates of the meetings were posted in the community on multiple occasions and sent home with students with the information in several languages. The meetings started with the principal giving an overview of how the year-round or modified calendar might work at their school. Then the group was divided into small breakout groups for discussion with translators available. This school principal stressed how important those meetings were. It was a chance for everyone to be heard.

Next, the annual back-to-school night event provides a large audience of parents to whom the proposal and survey of interest can be presented in order to determine the level of parental interest in a modified-calendar format. To improve parent turnout at schools where there are many limited English speaking parents and/or parents who are not accustomed to attending an evening "back to school" event, organizers may think about offering a free dinner at the school, such as Spaghetti Night, and have all materials translated into the native language(s) of the parents. Also, the availability of translators at the event can assist the faculty with parents' spontaneous questions.

The second year is a good time to organize several town meetings for families and interested community members where results of the research conducted during the prior year can be presented along with the outcomes of the parental survey. When the faculty has spent a prior year collecting information and understanding the benefits of a modified calendar, the town meetings are more constructive. It is important for faculty not to have a win-or-lose mentality during this phase, but rather to be open to hearing everyone's thoughts. Some parents will oppose the idea of year-round education, but once parents and community members have had a chance to learn about modified-calendar schools and what they can do for the students and teachers, consensus can be achieved. A final survey must be sent to all families. Generally, a two-thirds majority with 95 percent of parents responding is enough to constitute a mandate for adopting the year-round or modified calendar.

Finally, the principal should present the plan to the school board and superintendent. Be certain to include a prospective budget. Be candid about the additional costs and staffing requirements. Articulate the reasons for the change, and cite the results of the two years of research work done by the faculty. Emphasize the anticipated improvement of both academic and nonacademic outcomes for students and teachers as a result of the change. Also, discuss the results of the parental survey to show that parents strongly support a transition to the year-round education calendar.

At one case study school that was quite successful in ultimately gaining school board approval, the assistant principal was appointed during the second planning year to act as a liaison with the superintendent's office and the local school board member. The assistant principal kept the lines of two-way communication open to the new idea. She put it like this, "There was a tapestry being woven here. I was weaving constantly at the staff level, student level, parent level, community level, political level, state level, and bureaucratic level."

Another case study school was turned down by the school board because the board felt the school was not yet ready to transition. The school was given $13,000 from the district to continue planning and working through details. The school's patience ultimately paid off. In the following year, the school was granted permission to operate on the year-round or modified calendar "the next year."

Step Three

Once the school board approves the decision, the third year should be spent preparing for the transition. Coordinating and planning the upcoming intersessions is of chief importance. Many schools hire an intersession coordinator, who is usually a former teacher from that school.

Staffing considerations, such as hiring an intersession coordinator and intersession teachers, need to be addressed before the new modified calendar year begins. Also, support services performed by the custodial and cafeteria staffs, bus drivers, and school crossing guards must be aligned with the new calendar. Other important details include the preparation of district report cards and special education services as specified on individual education plans (IEPs).

Collecting baseline data from standardized test scores to compare after the transition is completed is highly recommended. Other useful baseline data might be: absenteeism figures for both students and teachers and the frequency of discipline referrals to the principal. A school calendar for the upcoming modified calendar year should be furnished to parents during the third year.

Also, it is important to remember that students and teachers will have a significantly shorter summer break the first year the school implements a year-round or modified calendar. For example, the traditional school year could end in June, and the alternative calendar year would commence August 1. That would only leave about four weeks for a summer break. This is a disadvantage voiced by many teachers.

PARENTS

Some literature on parental satisfaction with the year-round or modified calendar was based on interviews with mostly middle and upper-middle-class parents. Most of those parents who had prior experience with year-round or modified-calendar schools favored that calendar. They believed that the shorter summer vacation resulted in considerably less stress for the parents and less boredom for children during vacation time, better retention of learned material, and less education burnout for their children. Parents also found the breaks throughout the year to be a good time to take family vacations.

Parents and teachers alike agree that modified-calendar schools provide an educational option. Where a modified-calendar facility is the neighborhood or base school, most districts allow parents to choose a traditional-calendar school. Also, those parents felt that communication was better at a modified-calendar school, perhaps because the teachers are not as stressed. Immigrant parents showed preference for the modified calendar because of the longer winter vacation—the traditional ten to fourteen days and then a two-week intersession in January. The winter break is much favored for travel back to their native lands.

ADMINISTRATORS

Numerous principals in year-round or modified-calendar schools note that there are more teacher applicants for their schools because teachers like working in an environment that fosters interaction, collaboration, and systematic team planning. Also, the breaks, when spread throughout the year, lead to less stress, fatigue, and burnout, which may positively impact teacher attendance. This most likely saves the school funds on substitute teachers. Fewer incidences of school vandalism also are reported, perhaps because of an increase in school pride and school occupancy; the modified calendar leads schools to be unoccupied for shorter periods of time.

INTERSESSIONS

One of the reasons many schools change to a modified calendar is for the extra time in school that is provided through the intersessions. Practically all modified-calendar schools offer what are commonly known as intersession programs during the breaks between regular school sessions. The schools charge a small fee, usually $25.00 per intersession. Some schools have been successful in securing grant funding for intersessions. Most students are not required to attend intersession classes but are highly encouraged to do so for educational, social, and emotional remediation and enrichment purposes.

Diane Connolly (NAYRE conference presentation, 2004) recommends that intersession planning should begin one year before a school starts up an intersession program:[1]

1. Develop an intersession calendar for the months of October, January, and March. Try to think about what classes or courses will be offered and match with the supplies. Order the supplies such as paper, markers, paint, physical education equipment, cloth, yarn, etc.
2. Get the word out early to the community and families as to the dates and times of day that the intersession will be held, what classes will be offered, and how students will travel to and from school during [the] intersession.
3. Send the students home with a "student interest" survey on potential intersession topics. Poll school faculty on relevant topics for students, such as academics, sports, hobbies, and the arts.
4. Begin to develop a pool of prospective intersession teachers or

---

1. Reprinted with permission from Diane Connolly.

instructors. Possible staffing options include: retired teachers, maternity leave teachers, college professors, graduate students, community members, and the permanent faculty.

5. Begin to recruit and interview intersession teachers. Advertising may include local newspapers, county, district, and/or university publication(s), radio ads, community flyers, and the library bulletin board.

6. In the fall, present an orientation program for the hired intersession teachers. This includes supplying guidelines for preparing a display board that would advertise their intersession topic. This board helps students and parents understand what the intersession class offers before registering. Also, directions for preparing a course outline or curriculum outline must be provided to the teacher, so he or she can write a day-to-day planning of the goals, objectives, learning activities, and assessment(s) for the course. The assessment must be performance-based and include a rubric. For the teachers who are not in the education field, the terminology may be different and require clarification.

7. Emphasize to the instructors the importance of the design of the intersession classes and the need to be activity oriented, "hands-on" (no paper/pencil drill), student centered, and/or project-based. Also, contact the school transportation office and work through the busing of students to and from intersessions. Again, focus on the schedule and cost of this service.

8. Also, in the fall, student referrals for remediation and enrichment courses may be made based on standardized test scores, teacher identification, ESOL teacher referral, parental input, and other school committee referrals. Allow referred students to still have choices in remediation intersession classes and reduce class size for those courses.

9. Intersession brochures need to be developed and printed for students to take home. Be certain the brochures include a cover page, general information (time, place, etc.), courses at a glance, course descriptions, and a registration form (see appendix C for another school's brochure example).

10. The Intersession Teacher Workday should be scheduled to be held several days before the intersession begins. The meeting

with the intersession teachers needs to cover school security, fire drill procedures, lunch schedule, student emergency cards, discipline and student expectations, playground rules, medication lists for students, and any other relevant information.

11. After the intersession, instructors should have an opportunity to evaluate the execution of the intersession and offer feedback for future intersessions.

Another recommendation for a school that is just beginning to plan for intersessions is to have the core group (from step 1) visit a school that is operating intersessions successfully and is similar in student population, resources, and size. A list of year-round and modified-calendar schools is supplied in appendix A.

Partnering with Universities

The modified calendar, especially the intersessions, may lead to a variety of opportunities for university or college partnerships. For example, one of the schools in the case study placed local university practicum students in pairs to teach a two-week intersession course. The university practicum students developed a unit to teach in their social studies methods course and then implemented it during the intersession. A university supervisor or professor observed and monitored the practicum students during the intersession and gave them feedback.

This is a win-win situation since the university students have an opportunity to put theory into practice with their "own" classroom. The school benefits because the university students are not paid but rather receive field experience or practicum credit from the university. Another positive aspect for practicum students is that intersession classes are not so "high-stakes" in regards to curriculum pressure.

Another local university utilized an intersession to train practicum students in a field-based education course taught by the professor. The two-week October intersession was chosen due to the relative instructional freedom at the school and fewer curriculum pressures. The University professor agreed to teach a third and fourth-grade enrichment intersession course and developed a curriculum in social studies and language arts for Virginia history and folktales based on county and state standards.

During the two weeks, the professors' practicum students rotated into the class to observe their professor teach the children. In the second week, the practicum students had opportunities to coteach and be observed and evaluated by their professor. Overall, the administrators at the modified-calendar school were excited to have their students taught by university faculty and practicum students, which lowered the practicum student–pupil ratio. The school saved intersession funds because the practicum students supplied all of the materials for the lesson, which taught social studies through puppetry and the arts.

A partnership also benefits the university students since they are exposed through immersion to an alternative school calendar and to students in a high-needs environment. Other unique opportunities for university partnering include student teaching or internships beginning in the summer (August) and ending in early November before Thanksgiving and winter break—a busy time in K–12 and higher-education institutions. Also, applications for school–university grants may be easier to obtain through such a joint venture. For example, grants funds can be targeted for the funding of intersession classes where young students will concentrate their efforts on one topic, such as math remediation in a structured format.

GOING *BACK* TO A TRADITIONAL CALENDAR: WHY?

Many schools, particularly in Texas, that had switched to a year-round or modified calendar have switched back to a traditional calendar. According to the Texas Education Agency website (www.tea.state .tx.us/field/yre.html), enrollment in year-round education schools in 1997–1998 was 187,774 but declined to approximately 63,000 in 2002.

There are several reasons that schools in Texas and other states moved back to a traditional calendar after being on a year-round schedule. An overwhelming majority of schools that have returned to the traditional calendar have cited reasons that related to standardized test scores and operating costs. For many schools the increase in test scores was not dramatic enough to justify the additional costs of operating a twelve-month school. This included air-conditioning costs in August and June for schools in southern states such as Texas and Florida.

A retired principal of a school in Texas that was on a year-round schedule and then switched back to a traditional model said that a major part of the change back was the cost. "The school didn't have the appropriate funding to conduct intersessions that would help students. Also, test scores didn't increase fast enough for parents. The parents really wanted this [calendar] to have changes overnight and of course that didn't happen."

Some schools that have large numbers of students from military families found that these students tend to be regularly transferred and the modified calendar was difficult for them as they moved from or to traditional-calendar schools. Other reasons include communities that rely on high school students to fill jobs created by swelling summer tourist economies, as was the case in many Florida and Texas high schools. Those areas had the whole district (elementary, middle school, and high schools) on a year-round schedule, and the economic pressures forced the districts to move all grade levels back to a traditional calendar.

Also, unfortunately, divorce plays a part in districts' needs to educate students on a traditional calendar. At the urging of local courts, schools have considered the impact of parental custody for students during the summer months and found the year-round calendar to be difficult for those parents living out of the area or state. Responding to this need, many districts, particularly in the southwest, have moved back to a traditional calendar.

Providing consistency in special education programs and services on a year-round calendar was challenging for many schools and has prompted them to switch back to a traditional school schedule. Faced with the same challenge, all the case study schools in this book hired additional faculty or paid the current teachers an additional salary and met the IEP requirements during the breaks or intersessions.

In communities where parents provided stimulating opportunities over the summer such as camp experiences, music or other lessons, vacations, outings, excursions, and supervision of everyday play, there was sufficient parental influence to affect a change to a traditional calendar. Parents felt there was learning in the summer, just not "textbook" learning.

There were few high-needs or Title I schools that changed back to a traditional calendar after being a year-round or modified track. For the most part, the positive aspects of such a calendar for the needs of the student population far outweigh the negative. In many districts, including Fairfax County Public Schools, the only schools permitted to operate on a year-round schedule are schools that have lagging standardized test scores and a high population of English as a second language learners.

FROM THE CASE STUDY SCHOOLS: COMPARING ADMINISTRATORS' STYLES

The schools that were highlighted in the previous chapters had different reasons for becoming year-round or modified-calendar schools. Green Meadows switched to the alternative calendar because the teachers wanted a schedule that allowed students to have more time for curriculum. However, lagging standardized test scores drove New Garden and Westlake to transition to the alternative calendar.

Interestingly, all the principals from the case study schools implemented different administrative styles and behavior-motivation strategies. The transformational leading style of the first principal at Green Meadow was very constructive and supportive of the teachers and the school. The teachers led the way at all times throughout the process, and the principal was the guide or facilitator. The principal was an inspirational motivator because she wanted to support what the teachers were excited or passionate about. The principal had no hidden agenda or ulterior motives. Since the idea to adopt a modified calendar arose from the teachers, there was no pressure on the school, no expectations from the county. Previously, the county had never seriously considered a year-round or modified-calendar school in the system. At times, it seemed that the county's lack of expertise led the county administrators and school board members to raise more questions than answers for the teachers. Importantly, the teachers felt that the county did support them in achieving their goal.

The principal at New Garden embarked the teachers on her own idea from the beginning that the school would be a year-round or modified-calendar school. Early on, her chief mission was to bring teachers on board with the idea. Her administrative style was transformational and her motivational approach was goal setting with the ultimate goal for the school to switch to an alternative calendar.

New Garden's principal tried to replicate the transition process that Green Meadow went through. In fact, New Garden's principal said, "We followed the process that the pilot school [Green Meadow] went through. We received a lot of help from the [Green Meadow] assistant principal and parents who came to meetings and talked to our staff and community." Several teachers were sent to observe at the pilot school and reported their findings. Principals and teachers from both schools were united to help New Garden become a modified-calendar school in the county. Even the intersession coordinator from Green Meadow came to New Garden several times to help set up the first intersession.

At Green Meadow, teachers were more involved in the whole process of change. Teachers had ownership over the transition, while at New Garden teachers recognized that this was their principal's idea and they were to follow her lead or transfer to another school. Teachers, overall, felt her support in getting things done and in seeing to the instructional needs of the students. It is noteworthy, indeed, that none of the teachers expressed any resentment or disapproval over the fact that the principal was forceful in transitioning the school. On the contrary, they all admired her leadership style and her commitment and vision for the school. The only difference noted between the two teacher faculties was in the level of enthusiasm expressed by the groups regarding the transition. That difference was in part due to the Green Meadows teachers' feeling of ownership of the process versus the opposite at New Garden.

Support from county and school administrators, as well as fellow teachers, was a benefit that Green Meadow teachers enjoyed during and after the transition process. The principal who allowed the teachers to take control of the transition process facilitated the support. Although the other teachers at Westlake and New Garden schools expressed support, it was not nearly as strong since the principals at those schools had a different leadership style. Those school administrators were not seen as facilitators of teachers' desires in regards to transforming the school to a modified calendar.

The third case study school, Westlake, had a first principal who could best be described as somewhat authoritarian, which left the teachers upset and lacking faith in the democratic process of decision making at the school. There was poor communication or none at all between the principal and teachers as to the reasons for switching to a modified calendar. The teachers perceived that the reasons that the school was changing to the modified calendar were shrouded in mystery, which caused a great deal of stress and discomfort for the teachers.

However, a second principal came on board only several months into the first year of the modified-calendar school year. Her style of transactional leading was effective and appropriate for the situation. She wanted the teachers to trust her and have faith in the year-round or modified calendar, and those two goals needed to be met quickly. So she listened to teachers and asked them what they needed in terms of instructional support under the new calendar. She also took steps to improve their low morale. In return for meeting the teachers' needs, the principal was clear that the teachers needed to meet the children's needs, which would be reflected in the school's (higher) test scores. Many teachers immediately liked her and others grew to like her quickly in her first few months. They felt she was turning things around in an incredibly difficult situation.

Not surprisingly, three different schools with different leadership or administration styles transitioned into a modified calendar school with some similarity and dissimilarity. However, once all three schools were on the modified calendar for at least a year, the teachers were pleasantly surprised to find that the new calendar had numerous unexpected benefits for them as teachers.

SUMMARY

Changing over to a modified- or year-round calendar may be one avenue for schools when searching for a solution to several challenges embedded in a school—high teacher turnover and inadequate curriculum time in school for students, many of whom are ESL students or who come from lower economic backgrounds. Faculty responses at the schools researched for this book support the idea that teachers who have experienced both modified and traditional-calendar schools generally favored the modified calendar because of the breaks throughout the year, opportunities to teach intersession classes, and the availability of more instructional time in school for students, as well as other professional and personal aspects created under the year-round or modified calendar.

The "Single-Track" Year-Round or Modified Calendar

This calendar is devised so that the ten weeks of summer vacation is spread out more evenly throughout twelve months: four weeks in summer, two weeks in October, two weeks in January, and two weeks in March. Students attend at least the same number of days as their peers in traditional schools and have the same school holidays, such as winter and spring breaks. However, the intersession classes provide an opportunity for students to have up to thirty more days of instruction.

Teachers, especially those with less than three years of experience, felt that the breaks throughout the year provided a more balanced approach to their emotional needs, which contributed to a decrease in teacher absenteeism. Also, the breaks provided opportunities for off-season travel, something incongruous to a traditional-calendar school. Veteran teachers particularly enjoyed the freedom to travel abroad in October for two weeks when crowds are lighter, airfare prices are less, and weather is milder than in summertime.

The breaks throughout the year allowed teachers to focus on themselves and their families without the concurrence of a major holiday, which many felt attributed to a more emotionally balanced mental state. Teachers commented that the two-week breaks created new opportunities for gardening, visiting out-of-state parents, and tackling small home projects, such as gardening, which gave them an opportunity to step back from school and rejuvenate before returning for another nine weeks.

Several teachers who were taking courses online for a master's degree in education (M.Ed.) found the two-week breaks an ideal time to complete the majority of coursework without sacrificing too much vacation time.

The nine-week instruction format was better suited for thematic unit instruction, and teachers felt it was better for planning purposes, too. Also, the breaks after nine weeks allowed for careful consideration or professional reflection and implementation of new teaching methods, materials, and classroom management techniques that worked. Several teachers commented that others viewed the format outside of education as more "professional," since teachers were seen as "working" throughout the year.

INTERSESSIONS

The teachers felt that the intersessions yielded multiple positive factors for themselves and their students. First, teachers stated that the inter-session courses, especially remediation courses, supported their own teaching endeavors in the classroom. Many of the students in the three schools had little if any English spoken at home. The intersessions provided for a continuity of English language instruction and activities in a safe, stimulating, fun environment, which defeated summer learning loss. Also, teachers thought that "fresh eyes" provided by intersession teachers gave students a chance to learn from someone else and gave the students exposure to a different style of teaching.

Teachers who decided to teach an intersession course found many benefits as well. The additional salary was a financial incentive for many teachers. Other reasons cited by teachers who chose to work intersessions included the opportunity to teach a different grade level, different students, and share a beloved hobby, skill, or teaching method.

Team teaching and coteaching were additional perks that teachers found satisfying when working intersessions. It was a way to learn about other teachers' strengths in a casual, nonintrusive manner. When curriculum and testing pressures were deescalated, teachers found personal connections were made more easily and often carried over far after the intersessions were over.

Part-time teaching opportunities during intersessions were advantageous for those teachers on maternity leave or family leave. This was a way for them to stay in the teaching loop and keep their skills fresh. Permanent faculty who taught during intersessions liked working with others who were not on their staff. Again, it gave all teachers a chance to learn from others, and possibly gain new ideas and/or perspectives.

One of the most professionally rewarding benefits of teaching intersessions was the opportunity for teachers to structure and develop courses that utilized creative, hands-on methods. One teacher shared her intersession class, called "literacy chefs." Students read books like the *The Very Hungry Caterpillar* and then made "caterpillars on logs"—peanut butter and raisins on a celery stick. She mentioned that there was more time to focus on this literacy activity during an intersession than during the regular school time.

Students' Benefits

Teachers felt that the modified calendar supported the learning needs of their students, which aided their concerted effort in teaching. The remedial instruction offered to students through intersessions was a positive piece of the calendar that teachers overwhelmingly liked.

Also, the shorter summer vacation yielded a reduction in learning loss, which benefited both students and teachers. Teachers especially noted the decrease in English language loss when students had shorter breaks away from school.

Another positive aspect for students, according to teachers, was that the school was largely viewed as an integral part of the students' lives and their community. It was viewed as a safe, educational learning environment; a place where students wanted to be.

During the longer winter break (including the intersession) many immigrant families and their children travel back to the warmer climate of their native countries and the calendar permitted them not to be absent from school.

CHALLENGES

Delivery of special education services to those students with an Individual Education Plan (IEP) is a challenge many year-round or modified-calendar schools continue to face. Some schools hire special education teachers just for intersessions, and others pay the special education teachers from the school an additional salary to work during intersessions.

The first year that a school operates under the alternative calendar usually presents an unexpected challenge: after having only had three or four weeks of a summer break, teachers must be ready for students on or around August 1. Many teachers, despite being forewarned, feel "cheated" out of their summer break and not as mentally prepared to begin instruction in early August. Schools are trying to overcome this challenge by reiterating the "early return" in store for them during the first year on the alternative calendar. Also, schools are working to ensure that teachers and students who teach or enroll in summer school have at least four weeks of summer break before beginning on the alternative calendar in August.

CONCLUSION

Year-round and modified-calendar schools are not new; the idea began over one hundred years ago in the early part of the 1900s. However, the concept sprouted significant roots in the 1960s when more than 600 schools in twenty-eight states operated on this schedule. In the 1980s, the number dipped to approximately 300 schools, but by the 1990s, 1,800 schools (mostly elementary) in twenty-six states were established, with the majority located in California, Nevada, and Utah. By 2004, the number continued to increase with many more schools located in eastern and southern states as well as Canada. According to the NAYRE, since 1980, more than 3,000 schools have transitioned from a traditional calendar to a year-round model.

The need to raise standardized test scores in high-needs schools, which have a large percentage of ESL or ESOL students, will continue to be a chief reason as to why such schools switch to a year-round or modified calendar. However, merely reapportioning the breaks during the 180-day school year will not alone achieve to that end. Test scores will likely only increase at modified-calendar schools that adopt an intense literacy curriculum and conduct intersessions pursuant to county and state standards that require performance-based outcomes. Further, the intersession classes must be taught by effective instructors and overseen by a full-time intersession coordinator. If all of these conditions are met at a school, the teachers there will be more motivated to teach because their efforts in the classroom will be supported.

Appendix A

Year-Round Schools (www.nayre.org)

ARIZONA

Acacia Elementary School, Vail, AZ
Alta E. Butler Elementary, Phoenix, AZ
Anderson Elementary School, Chandler, AZ
Anderson Junior High School, Chandler, AZ
Basha Elementary School, Chandler, AZ
Basha High School, Chandler, AZ
Bogle Junior High School, Chandler, AZ
Canyon Breeze Elementary School, Avondale, AZ
Chandler High School, Chandler, AZ
Chandler Traditional Academy-Liberty Campus, Chandler, AZ
Chandler Unified School District, Chandler, AZ
Conley Elementary, Chandler, AZ
Copper King Elementary School, Phoenix, AZ
Crane School District, Yuma, AZ
Creighton Elementary, Phoenix, AZ
Creighton Elementary School District, Phoenix, AZ
Desert Mirage Elementary School, Glendale, AZ
Desert Sky Middle School, Tucson, AZ
Desert Willow Elementary School, Tucson, AZ
Discovery Elementary School, Glendale, AZ
Erie Elementary School, Chandler, AZ
Escuela Azteca, Phoenix, AZ
Esperanza Elementary, Phoenix, AZ
Estrella Mountain Elementary, Goodyear, AZ
Florence Unified School District, Florence, AZ

Fowler Elementary School District, Phoenix, AZ
Frye Elementary School, Chandler, AZ
Gateway Elementary School, Phoenix, AZ
Glendale American Elementary School, Glendale, AZ
Goodman Elementary School, Chandler, AZ
Hamilton High School, Chandler, AZ
Hartford Elementary School, Chandler, AZ
Hull Elementary School, Chandler, AZ
Humphrey Elementary, Chandler, AZ
Hyder Elementary School District, Dateland, AZ
Independence High School, Glendale, AZ
Isaac Middle School, Phoenix, AZ
Isaac Pre-School, Phoenix, AZ
Jacobson Elementary, Chandler, AZ
J. B. Sutton Elementary School, Phoenix, AZ
Joseph Zito Elementary, Phoenix, AZ
Keen Elementary School, Tucson, AZ
Kennedy Elementary, Phoenix, AZ
Knox Elementary, Chandler, AZ
Lake Havasu Unified, Lake Havasu, AZ
Lela Alston Elementary, Phoenix, AZ
Liberty Elementary, Buckeye, AZ
Liberty Elementary School District, Buckeye, AZ
Loma Linda, Phoenix, AZ
Machan Elementary, Phoenix, AZ
Mesquite Elementary School, Tucson, AZ
Mission View Elementary School, Tucson, AZ
Mitchell Elementary, Phoenix, AZ
Mohave Valley Elementary, Mohave Valley, AZ
Monte Vista, Phoenix, AZ
Morris K Udall School, Phoenix, AZ
Moya Elementary, Phoenix, AZ
Papago Elementary School, Phoenix, AZ
Pendergast School District, Phoenix, AZ
P. T. Coe Elementary, Phoenix, AZ
Pueblo Del Sol Middle School, Phoenix, AZ
Rainbow Valley Elementary, Buckeye, AZ

Rio Vista Elementary, Avondale, AZ
Sanborn Elementary, Chandler, AZ
San Marcos Elementary, Chandler, AZ
San Tan Academy, Chandler, AZ
San Tan K–8 Campus, Chandler, AZ
Shaw Elementary, Phoenix, AZ
Shumway Elementary, Chandler, AZ
Sonoran Sky Elementary, Glendale, AZ
Squaw Peak Elementary, Phoenix, AZ
Tarwater Elementary, Chandler, AZ
Tolleson Elementary School District, Tolleson, AZ
Tucson Unified, Tucson, AZ
Vail School District, Vail, AZ
Via de Paz Elementary, Phoenix, AZ
Weinberg Elementary, Chandler, AZ
Westwind Elementary, Phoenix, AZ

ARKANSAS

Cloverdale Elementary, Little Rock, AR
Elm Tree Elementary, Bentonville, AR
Fort Smith, Fort Smith, AR
Mabelvale Elementary, Mabelvale, AR
Mitchell Academy, Little Rock, AR
Stephens Elementary, Little Rock, AR
Woodruff Elementary, Little Rock, AR

CALIFORNIA

Alameda City Unified School District, Alameda, CA
Alameda High School, Alameda, CA
Alice Birney Elementary, Hollister, CA
Alvord Unified School District, Riverside, CA
Amelia Earhart Elementary, Alameda, CA
Anaheim City School District, Anaheim, CA
Antioch Unified, Antioch, CA

Antelope Crossing Middle School, Antelope, CA
Antelope Meadows Elementary, Antelope, CA
Apple Valley Unified School District, Apple Valley, CA
Arizona Middle School, Riverside, CA
Arlanza Elementary, Riverside, CA
Arroyo Vista Elementary, Chula Vista, CA
Auburn Union, Auburn, CA
Auburndale Intermediate, Corona, CA
Baldwin Lane Elementary, Big Bear Lake, CA
Bay Farm Elementary, Alameda, CA
Big Bear Lake Elementary School, Big Bear Lake, CA
Big Bear Lake High School, Big Bear Lake, CA
Big Bear Lake Middle School, Big Bear Lake, CA
Big Bear Unified School District, Big Bear Lake, CA
Blue Oak Elementary, Cameron Park, CA
Brentwood Elementary, Brentwood, CA
Brentwood Union School District, Brentwood, CA
Browns Valley School, Vacaville, CA
Buckeye Union School District, Shingle Springs, CA
Calaveras High School, San Andreas, CA
Calaveras Unified School District, San Andreas, CA
Caliente Union School District, Caliente, CA
Carroll Fowler Elementary, Ceres, CA
Casillas Elementary, Chula Vista, CA
Caswell Elementary, Ceres, CA
Ceres Unified School District, Ceres, CA
Chapman Elementary, Chico, CA
Charles Mack Elementary, Sacramento, CA
Chautauqua Continuation High School, Big Bear Lake, CA
Chico Unified School District, Chico, CA
Chino Valley Unified School District, Chino, CA
Chula Vista Elementary, Chula Vista, CA
Chula Vista Elementary School District, Chula Vista, CA
Chula Vista Learning Charter, Chula Vista, CA
Clear View Charter School, Chula Vista, CA
Clifford Cole Middle School, Lancaster, CA
Collett Elementary, Riverside, CA

Cooley Ranch Elementary, Colton, CA
Colton Joint Unified, Colton, CA
Cooper Elementary, Vacaville, CA
Corky McMillin Elementary, Chula Vista, CA
Corona-Norco Unified School District, Norco, CA
Discovery Elementary Charter, Chula Vista, CA
Donald Lum Elementary, Alameda, CA
Don Pedro Elementary, Ceres, CA
Dry Creek Elementary School, Roseville, CA
Dry Creek Elementary School District, Roseville, CA
Eastlake Elementary, Chula Vista, CA
Eastside Elementary School, Lancaster, CA
Eastside Union School District, Lancaster, CA
Edna Hill Middle School, Brentwood, CA
Emma Wilson Elementary, Chico, CA
Encinal High School, Alameda, CA
Edison Elementary, Alameda, CA
Elitha Donner Elementary, Elk Grove, CA
Elk Grove Unified School District, Elk Grove, CA
El Monte Elementary School District, El Monte, CA
Fairfield Suisun Unified School District, San Jose, CA
Feaster-Edison Charter School, Chula Vista, CA
Foothill Elementary, Riverside, CA
Florin Elementary School, Elk Grove, CA
Foulks Ranch Elementary, Elk Grove, CA
Foxboro Elementary, Vacaville, CA
Franklin Elementary, Alameda, CA
Frank Otis Elementary, Alameda, CA
Garin Elementary, Brentwood, CA
Glendale Unified, Glendale, CA
Gold Strike High School, San Andreas, CA
Grand Terrace Elementary, Grand Terrace, CA
Haight Elementary, Alameda, CA
Harriet Eddy Middle School, Sacramento, CA
Hawthorne Elementary, Hawthorne, CA
Heritage Elementary School, Chula Vista, CA
Heritage Oak Elementary, Roseville, CA

Holly Avenue Elementary, Arcadia, CA
Irvine Unified, Irvine, CA
Isabelle Jackson Elementary, Sacramento, CA
Island High School, Alameda, CA
James Rutter Middle School, Sacramento, CA
Jenny Lind Elementary, Valley Springs, CA
John Adams Elementary, Corona, CA
John Ehrhardt Elementary, Elk Grove, CA
Joseph Sims Elementary, Elk Grove, CA
Juarez-Lincoln Elementary, Chula Vista, CA
Jurupa Vista Elementary, Fontana, CA
La Granada Elementary, Riverside, CA
La Mesa-Spring Valley, La Mesa, CA
La Sierra High School, Riverside, CA
Las Palma Elementary, San Clemente, CA
Lauderbach Elementary, Chula Vista, CA
Lincoln Middle School, Alameda, CA
Little Chico Elementary, Chico, CA
Loma Verde Elementary, Chula Vista, CA
Loma Vista Elementary, Brentwood, CA
Loma Vista Middle School, Riverside, CA
Longfellow Elementary, Alameda, CA
Los Altos School, Chula Vista, CA
Los Angeles Unified, Los Angeles, CA
McAuliffe Elementary, Riverside, CA
McKinley Elementary, Bakersfield, CA
Maeola Beitzel Elementary, Sacramento, CA
Mary Tsukamoto Elementary, Elk Grove, CA
Michael D'Arcy Elementary, Fontana, CA
Miller Elementary, Alameda, CA
Montgomery High School, San Diego, CA
Myra Lynn Elementary, Riverside, CA
Neal Dow Elementary, Chico, CA
Nord Elementary, Chico, CA
Norte Vista High School, Riverside, CA
North County Elementary, Antelope, CA
North Shore Elementary School, Big Bear Lake, CA

Oakbrook Elementary School, Fairfield, CA
Oak Meadow Elementary, El Dorado Hills, CA
Olive Grove Elementary, Roseville, CA
Olympic View Elementary, Chula Vista, CA
Orange County School District, Orange County, CA
Orrenmaa Elementary, Riverside, CA
Oxnard Elementary, Oxnard, CA
Paden Elementary, Alameda, CA
Promenade Elementary, Riverside, CA
Quail Glen Elementary, Antelope, CA
Rail Road Flat Elementary, Rail Road Flat, CA
Redlands Unified, Redlands, CA
Riverside Unified, Riverside, CA
Robert Mueller Charter School, Chula Vista, CA
Rohr Elementary, Chula Vista, CA
Rolling Hills Middle School, El Dorado Hills, CA
Ron Nunn Elementary, Brentwood, CA
Rosedale Elementary, Chico, CA
Rosemary Kennedy Elementary, Riverside, CA
R. Paul Krey Elementary, Brentwood, CA
Sam Vaughn Elementary, Ceres, CA
San Andreas Elementary, San Andreas, CA
San Bernardino City Unified, San Bernardino, CA
Silva Valley Elementary, El Dorado Hills, CA
Silverado Middle School, Roseville, CA
Silver Wing Elementary, Chula Vista, CA
Stevenson Ranch Elementary, Stevenson Ranch, CA
Stockton City Unified, Stockton, CA
Stone Lake Elementary, Elk Grove, CA
Susan B. Anthony Elementary, Corona, CA
Sweetwater High School, National City, CA
Sylvan Union, Modesto, CA
Terrace Elementary School, Riverside, CA
Thurgood Marshall Elementary, Chula Vista, CA
Tierra Bonita North Elementary, Lancaster, CA
Tierra Bonita South Elementary, Lancaster, CA
Toyon Middle School, Valley Springs, CA

T. R. Smedberg Middle School, Sacramento, CA
Twin Hill Elementary, Riverside, CA
Union House Elementary, Sacramento, CA
Valley Springs Elementary, Valley Springs, CA
Valley View Elementary, Riverside, CA
Ventura Unified, Ventura, CA
Villegas Middle School, Riverside, CA
Virginia Parks Elementary, Modesto, CA
Vista Square Elementary, Chula Vista, CA
Vista Unified, Vista, CA
Walter White Elementary, Ceres, CA
Washington Elementary, Alameda, CA
Wells Middle School, Riverside, CA
West Contra Costa, Richmond, CA
West Point Elementary, West Point, CA
Westport Elementary, Modesto, CA
Whitmore Charter School, Ceres, CA
Will C. Wood Middle School, Alameda, CA
William Bristow Middle School, Brentwood, CA
Woodland Joint Unified, Woodland, CA
Woodstock Elementary, Alameda, CA
Yuba City Unified, Yuba City, CA

COLORADO

Barrett Elementary, Denver, CO
Bryant Webster Elementary, Denver, CO
Cheltenham Elementary, Denver, CO
Cherry Creek, Englewood, CO
Denver Public Schools, Denver, CO
Douglas County Schools, CO
Eagleton Elementary, Denver, CO
Eastridge Community Elementary School, Aurora, CO
Fairmont Elementary, Denver, CO
Johnson Elementary, Denver, CO
Maria Mitchell Elementary, Denver, CO

DELAWARE

Seaford School District, Seaford, DE

FLORIDA

Leon County, Tallahassee, FL
Pinellas County, Largo, FL

GEORGIA

Victory Charter School, Atlanta, GA

ILLINOIS

Lincoln Elementary School, Mundelein, IL
Riverton School District, Riverton, IL

INDIANA

Lafayette School Corporation, Lafayette, IN
Lincoln Elementary School, Columbus, IN
Lowell Elementary School, Indianapolis, IN
Julie A. Frazier-Gustafson, Purdue University (Research on YRE
    and Extended Year)

IOWA

Indianola Community, Indianola, IA

KENTUCKY

Bardstown City Schools, Bardstown, KY
Burgin Independent School, Burgin, KY

Eminence Independent School District, Eminence, KY
Jefferson County, Jefferson City, KY

LOUISIANA

Shreve Island Elementary, Shreveport, LA

MASSACHUSETTS

Salem School District, Salem, MA

MINNESOTA

Four Seasons Elementary, MN

MISSISSIPPI

Bell Accelerated Year-Round School, Boyle, MS

NEBRASKA

Meadowlark Elementary School, Kearney, NE

NEVADA

Clark County, Las Vegas, NV
Churchill County, Fallon, NV
Clyde Cox Elementary, Las Vegas, NV
Cortez Elementary, Las Vegas, NV
Ernest May Elementary, Las Vegas, NV
Garehime Elementary, Las Vegas, NV
Helen Herr Elementary, Las Vegas, NV
Richard Bryan Elementary, Las Vegas, NV
Washoe County, Reno, NV

NORTH CAROLINA

Adams Elementary, Raleigh, NC
Academic Heights Elementary, Pinehurst, NC
Baldwin Elementary School, Hope Mills, NC
Belville Elementary, Belville, NC
Benton Heights Elementary, Monroe, NC
Bolton Elementary School, Winston-Salem, NC
Brown Elementary School, Hope Mills, NC
Chestnut Elementary, Fayetteville, NC
Children's Center, Winston-Salem, NC
Craven County, New Bern, NC
Durant Road Elementary, Raleigh, NC
Durant Road Middle School, Raleigh, NC
Easley Elementary, Durham, NC
Easton Elementary, Winston-Salem, NC
E. E. Miller Elementary, Fayetteville, NC
Green Elementary, Raleigh, NC
Hall-Woodward Elementary, Winston-Salem, NC
Hendersonville Elementary, Hendersonville, NC
Heritage Elementary, Wake Forest, NC
Holt Elementary, Durham, NC
Kimberley Park Elementary, Winston-Salem, NC
Leland Middle School, Leland, NC
Lincoln Primary School, Leland, NC
Lufkin Road Middle School, Wake Forest, NC
McLauchlin (J. W.) Elementary, Raeford, NC
Meadowbrook Elementary, Canton, NC
Mineral Springs Elementary, Winston-Salem, NC
Monroe Middle School, Monroe, NC
Moore Square Magnet Middle School, Raleigh, NC
Morrisville Elementary, Morrisville, NC
New Hanover County, Wilmington, NC
Oak Grove Elementary, Raleigh, NC
Old Richmond Elementary, Tobaccoville, NC
Orange County, Hillsborough, NC
Pearsontown Elementary, Durham, NC

Petree Elementary, Winston-Salem, NC
Reid Ross Classical School, Fayetteville, NC
Riverside Elementary Magnet School, Louisburg, NC
Rockfish Hoke Elementary, Raeford, NC
Rockingham County, Eden, NC
Rogers-Herr Middle School, Durham, NC
Shiloh Elementary, Monroe, NC
Southeast Raleigh High, Raleigh, NC
Terresa Berrien Elementary, Fayetteville, NC
Timber Drive Elementary, Garner, NC
Upchurch Elementary, Raeford, NC
Wake County, Raleigh, NC
West Hoke Elementary School, Raeford, NC
West Lake Elementary, Apex, NC
West Lake Middle School, Apex, NC
Wilburn Elementary, Raleigh, NC
Young Howard Elementary, Fayetteville, NC
Youngsville Elementary, Louisburg, NC

OHIO

Dayton City, Dayton, OH
Frederick Douglass Elementary, Cincinnati, OH
Harold Schnell School, Carrollton, OH

OKLAHOMA

Sequoyah Elementary School, Oklahoma City, OK
Tulsa Public Schools, Tulsa, OK

OREGON

Portland Public Schools, Portland, OR

SOUTH CAROLINA

Beaufort County School District, Beaufort, SC
Beaufort Elementary School, Beaufort, SC

Beaufort Middle School, Beaufort, SC
Bluffton Elementary School, Bluffton, SC
Broad River Elementary School, Beaufort, SC
Homeland Park Elementary School, Anderson, SC
Lady's Island Elementary School, Beaufort, SC
Mossy Oaks Elementary School, Beaufort, SC
Port Royal Elementary School, Port Royal, SC
Robert Smalls Middle School, Beaufort, SC
Shell Point Elementary School, Beaufort, SC
Whale Branch Elementary School, Seabrook, SC
Whale Branch Middle School, Seabrook, SC

TENNESSEE

Greeneville City, Greeneville, TN

TEXAS

Mae Smythe Elementary School, Pasadena, TX
Mesquite Independent, Mesquite, TX
North East Independent, San Antonio, TX
Socorro Independent School District, El Paso, TX

UTAH

Bennion Elementary School, Salt Lake City, UT
Jordon, Sandy, UT
Meadlowlark Elementary School, Salt Lake City, UT
Parkview Elementary School, Salt Lake City, UT
Rose Park Elementary School, Salt Lake City, UT
Salt Lake City School District, Salt Lake City, UT
Whittier Elementary School, Salt Lake City, UT

VIRGINIA

Aberdeen Elementary, Hampton, VA
An Achievable Dream Academy, Newport News, VA

Annandale Terrace Elementary, Annandale, VA
Bassette Elementary, Hampton, VA
Bette Williams Elementary, Virginia Beach, VA
Buena Vista City Schools, VA
Cooper Elementary, Hampton, VA
Dogwood Elementary, Reston, VA
Falls Church High School, Falls Church, VA
Franconia Elementary, Alexandria, VA
Glascow Middle School, Alexandria, VA
Glen Forest Elementary, Falls Church, VA
Graham Road Elementary, Falls Church, VA
Lee Elementary, Hampton, VA
Merrimack Elementary, Hampton, VA
Parklawn Elementary, Alexandria, VA
Schoolfield Elementary, Danville, VA
Seatack Elementary, Virginia Beach, VA
Smith Elementary School, Hampton, VA
Spratley Middle School, Hampton, VA
Stuart High School, Falls Church, VA
Timber Lane Elementary, Falls Church, VA
Wythe Elementary, Hampton, VA
Young Park Elementary, Norfolk, VA

WASHINGTON

Garfield Elementary School, Yakima, WA

WISCONSIN

Congress Extended Year-Round School, Milwaukee, WI
Hackett Elementary School, Beloit, WI
Nathaniel Hawthorne Elementary School, Milwaukee, WI
River Trail School, Milwaukee, WI
Starms Early Childhood Center, Milwaukee, WI
Starms Discovery Center, Milwaukee, WI
Urban Waldorf Elementary, Milwaukee, WI

CANADA

Andrew Hunter Elementary, ONT
Calgary Board of Education, Calgary, CN
Kanaka Creek Elementary, BC
Petit Casimir Memorial, MAN
Trillium Lakelands District School Board, ONT

Appendix B

Interview Questions

The following are questions that directed the interview with teachers:

1. How long have you been at this school?
2. Why did your school change to a modified-calendar school? How long has it been a modified-calendar school?
3. What roles did the teachers, school administrators, county administrators, and parents have in the transition?
4. What benefits do you see in the modified calendar?
5. What challenges?
6. What would you tell someone about your school?
7. What would you most want to change about your school?
8. Anything else you care to add?

Appendix C

Intersession Brochure

An Example of an Intersession Brochure from One of the Case Study Schools follows.[1]

---

1. Reprinted with permission from Kathleen Freeman.

FALL INTERSESSION
October 12 - 22, 2004
Intersession Information !

Registration Times:
- ❖ Registration will take place at   on **September 13th, 14th, & 15th**. Students should bring their registration form and money to school to give to their teachers.
- ❖ Registration for classes will be on a first come-first serve basis.

Registration Fee:
- ❖ Registration is $25 per student or $5 per student for a student on free/reduced lunch.
- ❖ The fee must be paid in cash, or by money order.
- ❖ The fee must be sent in **with** the registration form.

Transportation:
- ❖ Buses will run on the same schedule as a normal school week.

Meals:
- ❖ Breakfast and lunch are served each day of Intersession.
- ❖ Prices are the same as the regular school year, including free/reduced prices.
- ❖ **The registration fee for Intersession does not include any breakfasts or lunches.**

SACC:
- ❖ SACC (School Age Child Care) will be available during Intersession.
- ❖ Only students **presently enrolled** in the SACC program may use this service during Intersession.
- ❖ If your child is already enrolled in the SACC program, please let the SACC Director know whether or not your child will be attending the Intersession. The SACC phone number is

Intersession Schedule

	Monday	Tuesday-Friday
Morning Classes	9:00-11:00	9:00-12:35
Afternoon Classes	11:00-1:20	12:40-3:40

School hours for Intersession are the same as a regular school week.

Fall AM Intersession Classes

Class #	Class Title	K	1	2	3	4	5
1	Language Arts Through Cooking	X					
2	*Fun with Letters and Numbers	X					
3	Fee Fi Fo Fum	X					
4	Dazzling Dinosaurs	X					
5	Art From the Start	X	X				
6	Reading is Sweet!		X				
7	Animal Houses		X				
8	The Solar System		X				
9	Tales of Space		X	X			
10	Sounds of Autumn		X	X			
11	Getting Acquainted with Jerry Pallotta and Mem Fox			X			
12	Around the World in Ten Days			X			
13	Mask Mania			X			
14	Keep Your Heart Happy			X	X		
15	Character Under Construction			X	X		
16	*Become a Math Wizard				X		
17	Beginning Origami				X		
18	Super Snacks for Super Students				X		
19	Picking Our President				X	X	
20	Historic Horses of Virginia					X	
21	Fashionomics					X	
22	*Wonderful Words				X	X	X
23	A Musical Timeline					X	X
24	The Mystery of Math					X	X
25	*Parklawn Intersession Orchestra					X	X
26	Monuments & Memorials					X	X
27	Basketball FUNdamentals I					X	X
28	Basketball FUNdamentals II					X	X
29	Chatting in Chinese					X	X
30	*WRITE Out of This World!						X
31	*Community Service						X

* Children with Invitations will be placed first in these classes.

Fall PM Intersession Classes

Class #	Class Title	K	1	2	3	4	5
36	Language Arts Through Cooking	X					
37	Dazzling Dinosuars	X					
38	Fee Fi Fo Fum	X					
39	*Young Scholars Explore Systems	X	X				
40	Art From the Start	X	X				
41	*Fun with Letters and Numbers		X				
42	Snazzy Spiders		X				
43	Reading is Sweet!		X				
44	Sounds of Autumn		X	X			
45	Tales of Space		X	X			
46	Super Snacks for Super Students			X			
47	Animal Houses			X			
48	The Solar System			X			
49	Treasures of the Deep			X	X		
50	A Musical Timeline			X	X		
51	Fashionomics				X		
52	Around the World in Ten Days				X		
53	Chatting in Chinese				X		
54	Basketball FUNdamentals III					X	X	
55	Basketball FUNdamentals IV					X	X	
56	Parklawn Publishers, Inc.					X	X	
57	Acting Your Way Through Colonial Virginia					X	
60	Advanced Origami						X	X
61	Character Under Construction						X	X
62	Kaleidoscope						X	X
63	The Mystery of Math						X	X
64	Fur, Fins, & Feathers							X
65	*The Power of Math							X
66	*Community Service							X

* Children with Invitations will be placed first in these classes.

Fall Intersession AM Class Descriptions

Kindergarten:

1. Language Arts through Cooking

Come investigate the world of Language Arts through cooking. Language Arts activities will include reading big books and poems, interactive and journal writing, and learning stations and centers . . . all with a cooking theme. We will prepare simple recipes reflecting the week's theme. The students will create a recipe and poetry book detailing their experiences.

2. Fun with Letters and Numbers! (Invitation First)

This course will reinforce your child's knowledge of the alphabet and the numbers up to thirty. They will be asked to count and record numbers of objects, while learning the concepts of addition and subtraction. They will compose their own stories through art. Stories, songs and games will add to the learning fun!

3. Fee, Fi, Fo, Fum!

Come explore the world of nursery rhymes and fairy tales! Through nursery rhymes and fairy tales students will compare and contrast, sequence, retell, graph, dramatize, create hands-on projects, and write about their experiences. Hop on for an exciting journey into the land of Once Upon a Time . . . !

4. Dazzling Dinosaurs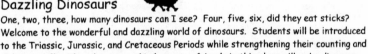

One, two, three, how many dinosaurs can I see? Four, five, six, did they eat sticks? Welcome to the wonderful and dazzling world of dinosaurs. Students will be introduced to the Triassic, Jurassic, and Cretaceous Periods while strengthening their counting and alphabet skills. The adventurous kindergarten friends in this class will make dinosaur eggs, cut and paste a Tyrannosaurus Rex, and make funny dinosaur hats.

Grades K & 1:

5. Art From the Start

This class will teach children some basic skills they will need to create their own art. Students will use skills such as cutting, pasting, drawing, coloring, and painting. Form and shape will be taught through drawing, pasting and assembling. Creating decorative letters will help students practice their letters while creating works of art!

Grade 1:

6.   Reading is Sweet!

It is October, and Halloween is just around the corner. You know what the best part of Halloween is? CANDY! Reading is just as sweet, especially if you are reading about candy! Have you ever wondered where candy comes from? How is it made, and can you make it yourself? Why does it taste so good, and why can't you eat it all the time? Do children all over the world eat the same kind of candy? In this reading class we will use books, word study games, videos, and our own experiments to answer all these candy questions and more!

7.   Animal Houses

Come explore different animals of the world! In this course we will discover where and how different animals live. We will also investigate ways to keep animals habitats from disappearing and keep animals from becoming extinct.

8.   The Solar System

Come explore our solar system! In this course students will learn about the nine planets that make up our solar system. They will learn details about life on these planets. Students will also learn about our star the sun, and other stars in the galaxy. So come take a trip into outer space and learn more about the planet you live on and it's neighbors!

Grades 1 & 2:

9.   Tales of Space

Do you know how many moons orbit the Earth? Come take a trip into outer space! We will explore our solar system and find out about the nine different planets and how they relate to each other. We will also learn about the four seasons and why the season change.

10.   Sounds of Autumn

Do you enjoy singing, moving, reading, and playing instruments? Music will be our guide as we explore the season of autumn in this class. We will learn and make connections through songs, poems, stories, writing, games, and other activities. Listen to the sounds that are all around you. Listen to the sounds of autumn!

Grade 2:

11. Getting Acquainted with Jerry Pallotta and Mem Fox

Join in the fun of learning about two great children's bookd authors, Jerry Pallotta and Mem Fox! We will read the books these authors wrote, complete art projects, sing songs, and participate in movement activities. Come improve reading for understanding, and creative writing skills while enjoying some wonderful stories!

12. Around the World in Ten Days

Students in this class will explore each continent's history, climate, geography, animals, and culture. Students will participate in a variety of activities from creating Ancient Canadian totem poles to participating in a World Cup soccer match. We will also have a guest speaker who will speak to us about birds and bats from around the world. This class will combine a wealth of knowledge, creative activities, and total submersion into the cultures of the world.

13. Mask Mania

Masks are not just for Halloween or birthday parties. Masks are used for celebrations and rituals throughout the world. Come on an exciting journey to many lands, near and far. We will learn about people who make masks, their customs, taste some yummy treats, listen and dance to music, and best of all . . . make our own masks!

Grades 2 & 3:

14. Keep Your Heart Happy

Students in this class will learn how the heart works and what it does. They will learn how to keep their heart healthy through exercise, nutrition, and a smoke free life. Students will also participate in physical activities to help them keep a happy and healthy heart!

15. Character Under Construction

This class will explore ways to be a good citizen. We will focus on six main pillars of character. We will write skits or plays, decorate posters, create scenery, and make crafts for others, all promoting good character. We will also play games and learn good sportsmanship all to help strengthen and build character. Do you have what it takes?

Grade 3:

16. Become a Math Wizard!   (Invitation First)

Amaze yourself with how well you will read, write, round, and compare 6 digit numbers. Add, subtract, estimate, and operate with numbers. Spend time on the Addition Fact Track . . . zoom, zoom! Increase your number power through fun math activities. Be SOL ready by playing games like "Three Truths and a Lie" and "Three False Facts". Come practice math using the computer and become a math wizard!

17. Beginning Origami

Origami is the "art of paper folding." This is the class for you if you want to make exciting projects with colorful paper. You will make animals, flowers, and dolls. You will also read and write about Japan, the culture that gave birth to the art of Origami. We will celebrate our learning with friends and family at our Origami Festival. So come learn a new art form.

18. Super Snacks for Super Students

Are you hungry after school? Would you like to make delicious, healthy snacks for yourself? This class will teach you how to read recipes and measure ingredients. You will make cheese quesadillas, banana bread, coconut fruit balls, tasty smoothies, tomato and cheese pizzas, and foods from many different countries. You will help create a mini cookbook with stories and pictures to go along with the different food recipes you learn! *NOTE: Children will be exposed to peanuts in this class.

Grades 3 & 4:

19. Picking Our President

Get ready for Election Day 2004! We will learn about the candidates running for President of the United States in the upcoming November election. You learn about the voting process, elections, and the job of the president. After taking this class, you may be ready to run for President yourself someday! Hail to the Chief!

Grade 4:

20. Historic Horses of Virginia

Have you ever wondered what it would be like to own a horse? The story or the horse goes back to the dawn of time, millions of years before the first people appeared on Earth. We won't be traveling that far back, but we will be going back in history to find out about some famous horses. These were special horses that belonged to well known Virginians. As you learn about the horses you will learn about part of Virginia's early history too. We may even have a 4-legged guest come visit us during our studies and help us prepare for the Virginia SOL's!

21. Fashionomics

 Do you love to shop or look at new clothes? Do you wonder why some clothes are so expensive or why they are always out of your size? Come learn how the latest fashions are made, bought and sold in Fashionomics! Come learn the art of supply and demand in the world of fashion!

Grades 3, 4 & 5:

22. Wonderful Words (Invitation First)

There are some wonderful words in the English language. In this class students will expand their vocabulary and word usage. Students will practice oral and written communication using these wonderful words. Students will play games, sing songs, and share stories.

Grades 4 & 5:

23. A Musical Timeline

Students will listen to, read about, and re-create musical masterpieces throughout history. They will learn about music and it's relation to different historical periods, along with its' relationship to the other arts. Students will be reading, writing, singing, playing instruments, dancing, and creating their own "production" of a musical timeline.

24. The Mystery of Math

In this class we will learn about addition, subtraction, multiplication, and division of whole numbers and steps to solve math problems. We will learn to add and subtract decimals through the thousands, as well as add, subtract, and multiply fractions. The students will learn to use problem-solving techniques to gain success in math. Come have fun with the mystery of math and learn to be a math success.

25. Parklawn Intersession Orchestra (Invitation First)

The students in Intersession Orchestra will learn in-depth music theory, music history, technique, intonation, and musical styles. They will also work on more challenging orchestral music.

26. Monuments and Memorials

Monuments, monuments everywhere! Why, how, who? Have you ever wondered who built the monuments we see everywhere around us? Have you ever wondered when they were built or why they were built? Now you can find the answers to these questions and more! Not only will you get the chance to read and write about these monuments, you will get to see them up close. You'll even get to design you own Parklawn Monument.

27. Basketball FUNdamentals I

In this class the FUNdamentals of basketball will be taught. We will do drills to practice shooting, passing, and defensive techniques. We will also learn more about the rules of basketball and some of its' players. Wear sneakers, bring your own water bottle, and come to have FUN!

28. Basketball FUNdamentals II

In this class the FUNdamentals of basketball will be taught. We will do drills to practice shooting, passing, and defensive techniques. We will also learn more about the rules of basketball and some of its' players. Wear sneakers, bring your own water bottle, and come to have FUN!

29. Chatting in Chinese

Come explore the fascinating Chinese language and culture. Through activities, drills, games, and projects, we'll learn about Chinese festivals, traditional stories, feng-shui, the Chinese zodiac, and common foods. Using Mandarin Chinese we'll learn to greet others, introduce ourselves, talk about our families, and even recognize some written Chinese letters called characters.

✏ Grade 5:

30. WRITE OUT of This World! (Invitation First)

Have you ever noticed how a good book really pulls you in and makes you feel like you are inside the story? In this class, we will take a look at how writers create the "world of the story", whether it is set in outer space, the wild west, or your fifth grade classroom. Also, we will read short stories and talk about the parts of a story, as well as the process of pre-writing and revising. So get ready for an opportunity to learn about reading and writing that will truly be "out of this world"!

31. Community Service (Invitation Only)

If you are chosen to participate in this class you will learn valuable skills for the working world. You will get hands on experience working with younger children while helping a teacher in a kindergarten and first grade classroom. You will keep a journal of all of your experiences and share all you have learned with other students in the program.

Fall Intersession PM Class Descriptions

Kindergarten:

36. Language Arts through Cooking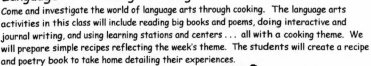

Come and investigate the world of language arts through cooking. The language arts activities in this class will include reading big books and poems, doing interactive and journal writing, and using learning stations and centers . . . all with a cooking theme. We will prepare simple recipes reflecting the week's theme. The students will create a recipe and poetry book to take home detailing their experiences.

37. Dazzling Dinosaurs

One, two, three, how many dinosaurs can I see? Four, five, six, did they eat sticks? Welcome to the wonderful and dazzling world of dinosaurs. Students will be introduced to the Triassic, Jurassic, and Cretaceous Periods while strengthening their counting and alphabet skills. The adventurous kindergarten friends in this class will make dinosaur eggs, cut and paste a Tyrannosaurus Rex, and make funny dinosaur hats.

38. Fee, Fi, Fo, Fum!

Come explore the world of nursery rhymes and fairy tales! Through nursery rhymes and fairy tales students will compare and contrast, sequence, retell, graph, dramatize, create hands-on projects, and write about their experiences. Hop on for an exciting journey into the land of Once Upon a Time . . . !

Grades K & 1:

39. Young Scholars Explore Systems (Invitation First)

Young scholars will gain greater understanding of systems all around them by exploring and collecting information. Young scholars will meet Leonardo Da Vinci, match fingerprints to a crime scene, and look at the many systems within their own bodies.

40. Art From the Start

This class will teach children some basic skills they will need to create their own art. Students will use skills such as cutting, pasting, drawing, coloring, and painting. Form and shape will be taught through drawing, pasting and assembling. Creating decorative letters will help students practice their letters while creating works of art!

Grade 1:

41. Fun with Letters and Numbers! (Invitation First)

Through the use of stories, songs, and games, this course will reinforce the student's knowledge of colors, shapes, patterning, and sequencing. Students will also practice letter and number recognition, counting, and the alphabet. The students will practice letter sounds and simple addition and subtraction concepts.

42. Snazzy Spiders

Students will explore the world of spiders while immersed in opportunities to develop language arts skills. Through a focus on David Kirk and his "Miss Spider" books, we will explore the work of an author. Students will develop greater understanding and knowledge of spiders through exploration activities, observation, and language experiences.

43. Reading is Sweet!

It is October, and Halloween is just around the corner. You know what the best part of Halloween is? CANDY! Reading is just as sweet, especially if you are reading about candy! Have you ever wondered where candy comes from? How is it made, and can you make it yourself? Why does it taste so good, and why can't you eat it all the time? Do children all over the world eat the same kind of candy? In this reading class we will use books, word study games, videos, and our own experiments to answer all these candy questions and more!

Grades 1 & 2:

44. Sounds of Autumn

Do you enjoy singing, moving, reading, and playing instruments? Music will be our guide as we explore the season of autumn in this class. We will learn and make connections through songs, poems, stories, writing, games, and other activities. Listen to the sounds that are all around you. Listen to the sounds of autumn!

45. Tales of Space

Do you know how many moons orbit the Earth? Come take a trip into outer space! We will explore our solar system and find out about the nine different planets and how they relate to each other. We will also learn about the four seasons and why the season change.

◐ Grade 2:

46. Super Snacks for Super Students

Are you hungry after school? Would you like to make delicious, healthy snacks for
yourself? This class will teach you how to read recipes and measure ingredients. You will
make cheese quesadillas, banana bread, coconut fruit balls, tasty smoothies, tomato and
cheese pizzas, and foods from many different countries. You will help create a mini
cookbook with stories and pictures to go along with the different food recipes you learn!
*NOTE: Children will be exposed to peanuts in this class.

47. Animal Houses

Come explore different animals of the world! In this course we will discover where and
how different animals live. We will also investigate ways to keep animals habitats from
disappearing and keep animals from becoming extinct.

48. The Solar System

Come explore our solar system! In this course students will learn about the nine planets
that make up our solar system. They will learn details about life on these planets.
Students will also learn about our star the sun, and other stars in the galaxy. So come
take a trip into outer space and learn more about the planet you live on and it's neighbors!

◐ Grades 2 & 3:

49. Treasures of the Deep

This class will focus on the number and location of oceans, types of oceans animals, and
their environment. In this class we will make a Big Book and make individual pop-up, flap,
or accordion books for Language Arts activities. We will also create art projects and
make an ocean animal puppet.

50. A Musical Timeline

Students will listen to, read about, and re-create musical masterpieces throughout
history. They will learn about music and it's relation to different historical periods, along
with its' relationship to the other arts. Students will be reading, writing, singing, playing
instruments, dancing, and creating their own "production" of a musical timeline.

Grade 3:

51. Fashionomics

Do you love to shop or look at new clothes? Do you wonder why some clothes are so expensive or why they are always out of your size? Come learn how the latest fashions are made, bought and sold in Fashionomics! Come learn the art of supply and demand in the world of fashion!

52. Around the World in Ten Days

Students in this class will explore each continent's history, climate, geography, animals, and culture. Students will participate in a variety of activities from creating Ancient Canadian totem poles to participating in a World Cup soccer match. We will also have a guest speaker who will speak to us about birds and bats from around the world. This class will combine a wealth of knowledge, creative activities, and total submersion into the cultures of the world.

53. Chatting in Chinese

Come explore the fascinating Chinese language and culture. Through activities, drills, games, and projects, we'll learn about Chinese festivals, traditional stories, Feng-shui, the Chinese zodiac, and common foods. Using Mandarin Chinese we'll learn to greet others, introduce ourselves, talk about our families, and even recognize some written Chinese letters called characters.

Grades 3 & 4:

54. Basketball FUNdamentals III

In this class the FUNdamentals of basketball will be taught. We will do drills to practice shooting, passing, and defensive techniques. We will also learn more about the rules of basketball and some of its' players. Wear sneakers, bring your own water bottle, and come to have FUN!

55. Basketball FUNdamentals IV

In this class the FUNdamentals of basketball will be taught. We will do drills to practice shooting, passing, and defensive techniques. We will also learn more about the rules of basketball and some of its' players. Wear sneakers, bring your own water bottle, and come to have FUN!

56. Parklawn Publishers

Parklawn Publishers Inc. will provide an authentic application of the writing process. Students will explore how reporters gather information from the world around them and use the writing process to publish news articles. Students will then have the opportunity to observe other classes and use the writing process to publish their own newsletter reporting the happenings and activities of the fall Intersession.

Grade 4:

57. Acting Your Way Through Colonial Virginia

Colonial times were a long time ago, about seventy years after Columbus discovered America. They began when some settlers came from Spain to live in a colony in America in the year 1565. Colonial times ended when the thirteen English colonies became the United States. What affects did tobacco and slavery have on colonial life? How did Africans, American Indians, and other European immigrants influence the culture of Virginia? Why did Virginia's capital move? In this class you will discover the answers to these questions through reading, writing, singing, and acting. You will learn songs and create a play that will be presented to the 3rd and 5th grades in the spring. Fourth graders, sign up for this great learning experience!

Grades 4 & 5:

60. Advanced Origami

If you have already taken a beginning origami class, you'll love Advanced Origami! In this class, you will extend your knowledge of paper folding by creating three-dimensional projects. You will make a variety of ornaments, or kusudama, geometric solids, and boxes. You will also broaden your understanding of Japanese festival culture by reading and writing about Japan. We will host a traditional Japanese festival at the end of Intersession to celebrate all we learned with friends and family.

61. Character Under Construction

This class will explore ways to be a good citizen. We will focus on six main pillars of character. We will write skits or plays, decorate posters, create scenery, and make crafts for others, all promoting good character. We will also play games and learn good sportsmanship all to help strengthen and build character. Do you have what it takes?

62. Kaleidoscope

Do you love art? Would you like to try writing some fun poems? How would you like to improve your thinking skills? Jump in and join us for a great experience! Listen to stories, write poems, and create some amazing art projects. Each day we will listen, read, write, and do art work. Some of our projects include pastel scarecrows, pattern pictures, and pop-up books. Come make new friends and learn something new!

63. The Mystery of Math

In this class we will learn about addition, subtraction, multiplication, and division or whole numbers and solve steps to solve math problems. We will learn to add and subtract decimals through the thousands, as well as add, subtract, and multiply fractions. The students will learn to use problem-solving techniques to gain success in math. Come have fun with the mystery of math and learn to be a math success.

Grade 5:

64. Furs, Fins, and Feathers

In this class we will study all the aspects of the animal kingdom. We will take a close look at domestic animals. In this class students will learn the importance of animals in our lives.

65. The Power of Math   (Invitation First)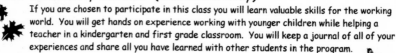

In this class you will sharpen your math skills and apply those skills and imagination to finding creative solutions to challenging word problems. Through reading, reflecting, and writing about the power of math you will learn the many ways mathematics has helped to create our man-made world of technology.

66. Community Service (Invitation Only)

If you are chosen to participate in this class you will learn valuable skills for the working world. You will get hands on experience working with younger children while helping a teacher in a kindergarten and first grade classroom. You will keep a journal of all of your experiences and share all you have learned with other students in the program.

INTERSESSION REGISTRATION FORM – Fall 2004

Registration must be received by 4:00 pm on September 15, 2004!
Non-Refundable Registration fee _must_ accompany this form.

Please return this form even if
your child will not be attending.

OFFICE USE ONLY		
D_____	C___	K____
M_____		A ____

Please list 1st, 2nd, and 3rd choices for each session. Confirmation of classes will be sent home Wednesday, **October 6, 2004.** Intersession dates are October 12 – 22, 2004.

PLEASE PRINT
Student's Name (first)_____(last)_____

Classroom Teacher_____   Grade_____

Parent's Name _____

Home Phone _____**Work Phone**_____**Other**_____

How does your child go home?
Walker____   SACC _____   Kiss & Ride _____   Bus Number _____   Other _____

☐   My child will NOT be attending this Intersession.
Parent Signature _____ Date _____

Morning (AM) Session: Monday 9:10 –11:20; Tuesday – Friday 9:10 – 12:35

	Course Title	Course Number
1st Choice	_____	_____
2nd Choice	_____	_____
3rd Choice	_____	_____

Afternoon (PM) Session: Monday 11:20 – 1:20; Tuesday – Friday 12:35 – 3:40

	Course Title	Course Number
1st Choice	_____	_____
2nd Choice	_____	_____
3rd Choice	_____	_____

ACCEPTABLE USE POLICY: I agree to follow all Parklawn rules concerning the use of computers and the internet during Intersession. These rules are stated in the Acceptable Use Policy that was returned to the school at the beginning of the school year.
Student Signature: _____**Parent Signature:** _____

Resources

The National Association for Year-Round Education (NAYRE)
  PO Box 711386
  San Diego, Calif. 92171-1386
  Phone: 619-276- 5296

www.nayre.org
www.nayre.org/related.html
  List of year-round and modified-calendar schools

www.nayre.org/year_rounder.htm
  The Year-Rounder, NAYRE's Electronic Newsletter

www.bctf.bc.ca/education/yrs/
  Research reports on year-round education by the British Columbia
  Teacher's Federation

www.ed.gov/databases/ERIC_Digests/ed378267.html
  Article from ERIC on implementing year-round education for overcrowded schools

www.catalyst-chicago.org/04-97/047opin.htm
  Commentary by the President of the National Association of Year-
  Round Education on year-round schooling in Chicago schools

www.educationalresearch.com/pages/projects/yrs/index.html
  A bibliography of studies and reports related to year-round
  schooling

www.pacpub.com/new/news/4-15-99/sbyearround.html
  Reviews of the feasibility of year-round schooling as a cost-saving
  measure

Literacy Collaborative at the Ohio State University
Literacy Collaborative Program
The Ohio State University
807 Kinnear Road
Columbus, Ohio 43212
www.lcosu.org
Phone: 1-800-678-6486

References

Atwater, D., and Bass, B. 1994. "Transformational Leadership in Teams." In B. M. Bass and B. J. Avolio, eds., *Improving Organizational Effectiveness through Transformational Leadership*, 48–83. Thousand Oaks, Calif.: Sage.

Ballinger, C. 2000. "Changing Time: Improving Learning." *High School Magazine* 7: 5–7.

Barber, J. 1996. "Year-Round Schooling Really Works." *Education Digest* 6, no. 22: 31–35.

Bass, B. 1985. *Leadership and Performance Beyond Expectation*. New York: Free Press.

Burns, J. 1978. *Leadership*. New York: Harper & Row.

Campbell, W. 1994. "Year-Round Schooling for Academically At-Risk Students: Outcomes and Perceptions of Participants in an Elementary Program." *Journal of School Research and Information* 12, no. 3: 20–24.

Capps, L., and Cox, L. 1991. "Improving the Learning of Mathematics in Our Schools." *Focus on Exceptional Children* 23, no. 9: 1–8.

Cohen, F., Cordi, T., Kitchen, B., and Ryan, M. 2000. *From Teacher to Teacher: A Look at Year-Round Education*. California: National Association for Year-Round Education publication.

Connolly, D. 2004. "Nuts and Bolts of Intersessions." Presentation to the Annual Conference of the National Association for Year-Round Education (NAYRE), San Diego, Calif.

Czubai, C. 1996. "Maintaining Teacher Motivation." *Education* 116, 3.

Davies, B., and Trevor, K. 1999. "Improving Student Learning through Calendar Change." *School Leadership and Management* 19: 359–71.

Ellis, T. 1984. "Motivating Teachers for Excellence." ERIC Clearinghouse on Educational Management." *ERIC Digest* 6.

Elsberry, J. 1992. "An Evaluation of the Implementation of Year-Round Education." Ph.D. diss., University of Texas at Austin. *Dissertation Abstracts International* 53, no. 4146.

Feistritzer, C. 1986. *Profiles of Teachers in the U.S.* Washington, D.C.: National Center for Education Information.

Frase, L. 1993. "Maximizing People Power in Schools: Motivating and Managing Teachers and Staff." *Effective Leadership* 5: 12–19.

Gandara, P. 1992. "Extended Year, Extended Contracts: Increasing Teachers' Salary Options." *Urban Education* 27, no. 3: 229–47.

Gandara, P., and Fish, J. 1994. "Year-Round Schooling as an Avenue to Major Structural Reform." *Educational Evaluation and Policy Analysis* 16, no. 1: 67–85.

Gardner, H. 1983. *Frames of Mind: The Theory of Multiple Intelligences.* New York: Basic.

Glines, D. 1995. *Year-Round Education: History, Philosophy, Future.* San Diego, Calif.: National Association for Year-Round Education; Saline, Mich.: McNaughton & Gunn.

Glines, D., and Bingle, J. 2002. *National Association for Year-Round Education: A Historical Perspective.* San Diego, Calif.: NAYRE Publications.

Haser, S., and Nasser, I. 2003. "Teacher Job Satisfaction in a Year-Round School." *Education Leadership* 60, no. 8: 65–68.

Hall, R. 1962. "The Concept of Bureaucracy: An Empirical Assessment." *American Sociological Review* 27: 295–308.

Herzberg, F. 1966. *Work and the Nature of Men.* New York: Crowell.

Hoy, W., and Miskel, C. 1996. *Educational Administration: Theory, Research, and Practice.* New York: McGraw-Hill.

Kneese, C. 1996. "Review of Research on Student Learning in Year-Round Education." *Journal of Research and Development in Education* 29, no. 2: 60–72.

Kocek, J. 1996. "The Effect of Year Round School on Teacher Attendance." ERIC Document. Cited in E. Palmer, and A. Bemis, 1999. *Year-Round Education.* University of Minnesota Extension Services.

Kotter, J. 1990. *A Force for Change.* New York: Free Press.

Lewis, D., and McDonald, J. 2001. "How One School Went to a Year-Round Calendar." *Time and Learning,* January, 22–25.

Locke, E., and Lantham, G. 1990. *A Theory of Goal Setting and Task Performance.* Englewood Cliffs, N.J.: Prentice-Hall.

Loyd, C. R. 1991. "Impact of Year-Round Education on Retention of Learning and Other Aspects of the School Experience." Ph.D. diss., Texas A & M University. Dissertation Abstracts International 52: 10-A.

Luce, J. 1998. "Career Ladders: Modifying Teachers' Work to Sustain Motivation." *Education* 119, no. 1: 15–19.

Nasser, I., and Haser, S. 2002. "Year-Round Education and Teacher Motivation: A Case Study of One Public Elementary School." *Education Research Service, ERS Spectrum*, Summer, 19–24.

Palmer E., and Bemis, A. 1999. *Year-Round Education.* University of Minnesota Extension Services. www.extension.umn.edu. Retrieved on October 31, 2003.

Parkaway, F., Olejnik, S., and Proller, N. 1988. "A Study of the Relationships among Teacher Efficacy, Locus of Control, and Stress." *Journal of Research and Development in Education* 21, no. 4.

Shields, C., and LaRocque, L. 1998. "Year-Round Schooling: A Catalyst for Pedagogical Change." *Alberta Journal of Educational Research* 44, no. 4: 366–82.

Shields, C., and Oberg, S. 1999. "What Can We Learn from Data? Toward a Better Understanding of the Effects of Multitrack Year-Round Schooling." *Urban Education* 23, no. 2: 125–54.

Smith, M., and Bourke, S. 1990. "A Contextual Study of Teacher Stress, Satisfaction, and Workload." Paper presented Australian Association of Research in Education. In A. Latham, 1998. "Teacher Satisfaction." *Educational Leadership* 55.

Southward, S. 2000. "Wanted: Two Million Teachers." *Instructor,* January–February, 25–27.

Warrick-Harris, E. 1995. "Year-Round School: The Best Thing Since Sliced Bread." *Childhood Education* 71: 282–87.

INDEX

About the Authors

Shelly Gismondi Haser is an associate professor in the School of Education and Human Services at Marymount University in Arlington, Virginia. Her background is in elementary and special education in high-needs Title I schools located in Washington, D.C., and the Fairfax County Public School system. Currently, she is the program coordinator for the Marymount University/Fairfax County Professional Development Schools program and a supervisor for Marymount University student teaching interns in clinical field experiences. She also teaches graduate courses in elementary social studies methods and special education.

Ilham Nasser is an educator who has spent over twenty years in teaching and research in different universities. She has also been training teachers and educators. Her main area of expertise is child development and early childhood education. Currently she is a visiting researcher at the Center for Global Peace at American University in Washington, D.C. where she is directing evaluation projects in education and teacher training.